Liber

Liberation into Orgasm

Through Pleasure Beyond Pleasure

Sofia Sundari

1

Liberation into Orgasm

•

Artist credit:
Sami Jo Giesel
www.omheartist.com

Cover photo by:
Bibbie Friman
www.bibbiefriman.se

Editor
Alba Brunetti

Graphic Design
Fleassy Malay
www.bodhidesigns.com.au

Table of Contents

Liberation into Orgasm

Thank you for dedicating your time to going on this journey with me. To express my gratitude, I would love to invite you to an event I will be holding, at no cost. It is called Liberation into Orgasm Lab. You can join it from anywhere in the world - it is going to take place online. There you will have the chance to ask me any questions about your orgasmic life, so we can go even deeper together.

Find out information and claim your spot here:
http://sofiasundari.com/liberation-into-orgasm

Love,
Sofia Sundari

Liberation into Orgasm

To my Beloved Reader:

I welcome you on this journey to expanded pleasure, expanded orgasms and to an expanded Life.

This book is for those who are either intrigued by sex but feel a little shy and perhaps have never experienced an orgasm, and for those who are very open yet have the intuition that there must be more to sexuality.

And forgive me for running ahead, but yes, there is always more to sexuality.

This book is for those who have endless spiritual thirst and those who wish to feel more connected to their true Self in every moment of their life.

In the modern day world, we tend to think that sex and spirit are separate from each other. Or, that in order to access the spirit, we need to transcend sex.

With this book, I want to serve the healing of the split that we have created between sex and spirit. This split is what causes disconnection, shame, guilt and judgment around something that is the most powerful creative force that moves through human beings — our sexual energy.

With this book, I want to reveal the tantric perspective of what is really possible for each human being in this Life.

With this book I want to invite you on a journey that will take us through pleasure beyond pleasure.

Tantra teaches us to live fully.

When someone chooses the path of Tantra, it means they choose to go all the way. To live Tantra means not to shy away from any of the aspects of our life. We see everything as energy, and we embrace even those shadowy parts of our consciousness, because we know that everything holds the key to infinite awareness, that is who we truly are.

It is said that tantrics may go all the way to the land of demons and from there extract the nectar of immortality.

Although Tantra is a very suitable path for modern people, Real Tantra is not for everybody. It is not for the masses, only for a select few people, those who are able to recognize the endless beauty of this path. The fact that you are now reading this book means that your soul is ready for this information. Receive it to the fullest.

You will notice that many times in my writing it is implied that I am referring to a heterosexual relationship. I use this model to simplify things. But a lot of what is written in this book equally aligns with homosexual relationships as well, as we all carry the masculine and the feminine within us.

Liberation into Orgasm

1
Meet the Heroes: Eros, Sex and Orgasm

What Is Eroticism?

When we allow ourselves to feel Life, to feel what it means to be deeply alive, we can't help but feel the erotic nature of it. Life is infused with eroticism. Eroticism is as natural as life is. Eroticism is our natural state and it does not imply that something needs to be done with it or about it. The deepest purest essence of life is erotic. Look at babies and little children. Look at the way they throw themselves into Life. They are so naturally and beautifully erotic. They are comfortable living in their bodies. They love to cuddle, and to open their bodies to the sun and wind. And there is nothing dirty or kinky about it. It is simply natural and beautiful. At around the age of three or four, children develop an interest in their genitals. They naturally want to explore and touch themselves. At this point in most case something very significant happens: children are told that it is wrong to touch themselves.

Eros is not about what we do. It is a space that we enter. Eros is not limited to sex, but it includes and embraces sexuality.

What Is Sex?

Sex and sexual energy are potent portals to Eroticism.

We are conditioned to have very specific ideas about what sex should look like and what pleasure should feel like. For many, sex is all about thrusting, sweating, pumping and humping. Then reaching a peak (hopefully), cuddling a little (maybe), smoking a cigarette and falling asleep. This is a mainstream view of sex. This is what we learn from movies, porn and other "sexual education sources" available out there. Yes, for most of us pornography is the only source of sexual education. And it represents no more than 2% of what sexuality really is. This is really pathetic. What most people associate with sexuality, with erotic and therefore, with orgasm, is only a tiny little fraction of what it really is.

Sex has enormous power. That's why no one is neutral about sex. Everyone has strong opinions and beliefs. It is part of our culture. Our culture is confused about sexuality — and largely obsessed with it. There is a lot of shame around this subject.

Even now, while reading this, I am sure many people will feel uncomfortable.

From our childhood, we learned that sexuality was shameful.

14

How many of us had been encouraged to explore our sexuality and learned to be ecstatic? How many were shamed for asking questions or (God forbid) touching ourselves?

Religion implies that our bodies are bad and sinful, and they need to be transcended.
Media uses sex to sell anything from fruit juice to cars.

All this is limiting people's understanding of what sex is really about.

Holding hands is sexual. Nature is extremely sexual — look at flowers or trees.
Sexuality is everywhere! Perhaps it is not in the form that most people associate it. In fact, sexuality doesn't even have to involve the genitals.

We did not receive any sexual education and were not given the skills to access our pleasure and own our orgasms because it is not something that society encourages or even approves.

From my experience educating people on the nature of sexuality and pleasure, I see that it's an exception to meet a woman who can orgasm freely — a big exception.

Most women either never have an orgasm with a partner, or have occasional five-second long clitoral peaks.

When we are at peace with sexual expression, sexual energy flows freely. But when we are imprinted with the notions of taboo and secrecy around sex — awkwardness and repression are created. In fact, violence and sexual abuse are nothing but

15

the result of sexual repression.

If as a society we didn't hold sexuality as something secretive, if we spoke about it openly, and view it as nothing but a healthy expression of love, there wouldn't be so much distortion and unhealthy repression around it.

Each of us can play a role in reversing the repression of sexuality. When we put an end to the shame around sexuality, we can dismantle the violence that occurs.

We need to take responsibility for the connection that we have with our own sexuality and heal ourselves from the shame, repression and disconnect.

It's the legacy of shame that has been passed down from our parents and grandparents for centuries that we carry today. It is that feeling that there is something embarrassingly wrong about us and there is nothing that can be done about it.

We can choose to re-establish an authentic connection to our body. We can reconnect our body, mind, heart and spirit with our sexuality.

We can realize that sexuality is a huge part of our lives. Sexual energy is the fundamental energy of a human being.

We can learn to harness it and direct it, instead of letting it get stuck and confuse us.

Look out for people who are deeply in touch with their sexuality.

They are rare and they always stand out in a crowd. These are people who are in their bodies, who feel incredibly alive. These people remember how it feels to be untamed, wild and free. These are the people who shine. They are naturally magnetic, and it makes you want to be in their presence.

What Is Orgasm?

Normally people imagine orgasm to be an intensely pleasurable peak few seconds, when you contract your body, followed by a release and relaxation.

In reality, the degree and depth of your orgasm depends on how open you are to Life.

Orgasm can happen on multiple levels: physical, energetic, emotional, mental and the level of consciousness. Either on one level at a time, or – on all levels simultaneously.

In orgasm, we can open as the sky, open as the entire cosmos, experience connectedness with everything and experience ourselves beyond ourselves.

A five-second peak experience of release pales in comparison to the real meaning of full orgasm.

Orgasm can be something like a genital sneeze or it can be something that expands you beyond what any kind of chemical, plant or drug can do to you. Through orgasmic expansion it is possible to be constantly high on life. It is also possible to be in an orgasmic state of being, when full-body orgasms happen outside of sexual encounters.

Eros is the energy of life. Orgasm is the flower of life.

I could not orgasm freely until I was 24. I really wanted to, though. I was researching orgasms on the internet, reading about other women's experiences, I was trying to move my hips faster during sex... Nothing worked.

Later I realized that I was too fixed on what I was expecting to feel so I was bypassing my actual experience, and therefore – opportunity to go deeper into my pleasure.

We need to stop having expectations on what a good orgasm should feel and look like so we can open ourselves to a deeper experience.

I see a direct correlation of orgasmicness, our ability to achieve deep and powerful orgasms, to someone's spiritual progress. As we cultivate orgasmicness, we are actually working on very subtle layers of our energy. The more we experience those tantric orgasms, the lighter our energetic body becomes. The energetic pathways are no longer blocked and the orgasmic energy flows freely through the body. There is a sense of ascension in the being.

Sex Free of Agenda. Sex Free of Performance.

As long as I remember, I've always been fascinated by sex. And I felt that there was much more to sex than how it's normally experienced. Only when I discovered Tantra did I start tapping into the power of the erotic. I went from experiencing hardly any orgasms at all to being highly orgasmic. The longer I am on the tantric path, and the deeper I go into the exploration of my sexuality, the more profound states of consciousness I experience through deepening in my eroticism.

I want erotic liberation for our human race. I want people to be erotically free. What this means is opening up to Life. It means making peace with the fact that we are sexual beings. Sex is what created us, sexual energy created this Universe, it is the fundamental force that moves us all. In fact, we could always be in a state of orgasm if we were not blocking it! Why would we block it, you may wonder.

Often it feels like modern life is designed in such a way to disconnect us from our erotic and orgasmic nature.

We are surrounded by technology, synthetic materials that don't allow energy to flow, artificial foods that pollute our system and then instead of naturally enjoying pleasure, our system needs to work hard to eliminate toxins. We are unconscious about our food choices. For example, not many people know that garlic is an antibiotic and if we take it on a regular basis we desensitize our system, and therefore, it affects our orgasmicness. The same is true for raw onion too.

Modern people are living in the mode of doing and not in the mode of being. Eroticism is about being. We are also mostly stuck in our heads; thinking, remembering, comparing, planning, calculating, strategizing and are completely disconnected from the present moment, and therefore, from Life.

19

It is only when we are in the now that we can experience pleasure and orgasms.

We can realize that the nature of our energy is flow. The nature of our energy is pleasure. If only we allow ourselves to sink deeper into each moment, we realize that life is pleasure.

In fact, our body is orgasmic by its very nature!

So where does our orgasmicness go? The connection to ourselves doesn't go anywhere, but oftentimes it is hidden under layers and layers of conditioning — our own, that of the society or the environment we grew up and/or live in. Are you feeling connected to yourself? Are you feeling deeply in tune with your sensual and erotic nature? Most people don't. Yet, this connection is your natural state of being.

2
A Very Brief Introduction to Tantra

Tantra is an ancient spiritual path, a lifestyle. It is a system of self-development in which sexual energy and desire is not suppressed, but it is harnessed and used for our spiritual unfolding.

More and more, Tantra is becoming something that people have heard about, experienced or practiced. Some people even know that it is not really about sex. Although sex, of course, is an important part of it, especially in modern times. This is simply because sex is everywhere anyway. Even people without any energetic awareness sense that there is something potent about sexuality. That's why many are either repressing it, or are controlled by their own sexual desires.

Tantra, in fact, is an ancient path to God. It is a path that is as extremely beautiful as it is challenging. This is because in Tantra we are not hiding from anything. Anything. We perceive everything as energy. We embrace the energy of intense feelings, such as anger, grief, sadness, and we also embrace desire,

21

sexuality, eroticism and orgasm. Tantrics know that none of the energy is intrinsically bad or good. It is just energy.

In Tantra, energy is seen as Shakti, the Divine feminine. It entails the entire manifest reality. Shakti is the feminine aspect of the Divine - the Goddess. The space where the manifest unfolds is seen as Shiva, the Divine masculine, or pure presence.

An important characteristic of Tantra is that unlike traditional spiritual paths it sees the sacredness not only of the Spirit, but also of the matter. Therefore, Goddess worship is a major aspect of Tantra.

There are two major paths in Tantra: Right-hand Tantra and Left-hand Tantra.

Right-hand Tantra does not include physical sexuality. It is highly symbolic and based on ritual. The study of 64 classical arts is part of right-hand Tantra. Practitioners of right-hand Tantra don't even need to touch each other to enter into profound states of consciousness. It is said that the intensity of their feeling and presence alone can make flowers blossom. Practices such as yoga, studying of Sanskrit, meditation, singing and other arts are part of right-hand Tantra.

Left-hand Tantra may or may not include physical sexuality. Left-hand Tantra is in its turn divided into white, red and black Tantra.

White is the color that symbolizes purity. In white Tantra, we work with energy and we aim to accumulate a lot of energy, but only to use it for our spiritual unfolding and for our ultimate liberation.

Red Tantra is where it starts to get dangerous. Since we are working with large amounts of energy and the pleasure that we can experience through tantric practice is really extraordinary, there is a danger of slipping and getting lost in sexual pleasure. For example, if we merely practice Tantra to sensually please our partner and we forget what it is really all about, we forget to move the energy to the heart and to use it for our awakening. We are not growing in spirit, and that means we are not actually practicing Tantra.

Black Tantra has to do with black magic. When we know how to accumulate and move our energy, we become incredibly powerful. It is very important that we have a very high level of integrity and our level of consciousness is high. I believe that the fact that you are reading these words means that you are ready for that and will not misuse the knowledge that you are acquiring.

I will be honest with you, at times it feels like in Tantra we walk on the edge of a razor blade. In Tantra, we choose to live fully — to live totally. It's as if Tantra is telling us: enough half-assing and holding back. What are we holding onto anyway? Living each day as the last one — this is when we get the opportunity to wake up. That's the way I choose to live my life, participating fully. At the same time, using each moment, each feeling, each encounter as a gateway to a deeper presence, to the real me.

Tantra teaches us that there is really no end to the depth of erotic opening. Even though someone may seem totally erotically free, there is always more. We need to stop defining sex and projecting our expectations onto what is a good orgasm. Because essentially, what we are opening to is our true Self. It is the Universe. It is a space of no separation. It is God. Yes, we can get there through sex. All that is available to you.

Exciting? I know! Read on.

The Tantric Outlook on Desires

Tantra is an incredibly suitable spiritual path for a modern-day person. In traditional spirituality, we often hear that we need to detach from our desires because our desires are endless and they make us hook into the material world. So, it is said that we need to transcend them. Unfortunately, what often happens is that in trying to transcend these desires, people simply suppress them. However, when something is suppressed it is not gone. It stays in our field and when energy is repressed, it usually manifests as disorder or even illness.

Tantra offers us an alternative. Tantra says that in order to detach ourselves from desires and transcend them, we actually need to find those very deep core desires and fulfill them. Once they are fulfilled, they stop carrying such a strong charge and then we are able to let them go.

3
Sex and Shame

What are the concepts and morals that we grow up with in regards to sexuality? What are the beliefs ingrained in society?

First of all: "Sex is shameful." It is something that cannot be discussed openly. It is something that's done behind closed doors and curtains, with the lights off, with your eyes closed and as quickly as possible. If your children ask about it (God forbid) give them as vague an answer as possible, so hopefully they will lose interest and forget about all these dirty perverse things altogether.

It is an exaggeration, but does reflect some truth.

At the same time, 80% of sex happens in people's imagination. This is statistically proven. 80%. Can you imagine? Imagine how much more radiance would be in this world if we would allow all that sexual energy to flow, rather than keeping it stagnant in our pelvis and have all the juicy action in our minds alone?

I don't think there is one other subject that has more shame around it than sex. Since it is such a fundamental aspect of our lives, this very shame affects all other arenas of our human existence. I'm not intending to come up with a radical solution that will heal humanity from shame once and for all. But, I know that each of us is responsible for this. Each of us can take steps to come to peace with our own sexual nature, our desires and our fantasies. Each of us can start to own our erotic longings and disentangle ourselves from the societal taboos and stereotypes of what it means to be decent. This choice is profound. It's up to us to do the work.

Even after years of work, sometimes you may encounter new layers of shame. It is a process that I've been witnessing within myself. This shame is not sticky anymore. It doesn't stay. Whenever it comes up, I recognize it, I feel into it, I move the energy and it goes. I am no longer identified with it. And it's very liberating.

Once we refuse to cage ourselves inside limiting concepts, a very big space within us opens up and allows incredible light to shine through. This light touches everyone around us.

This light is healing this world.

4
Reframing Orgasm

To understand the potential of the pleasure that our body is capable of we need to shift from the narrow view of an orgasm. What do you visualize when you hear the word "orgasm"? Most probably, you think of a sharp pleasurable sensation in the genitals that makes your body tense up, followed by a release. This is called **peak orgasm**. It is only **a** type of orgasm.

The tensing up of the body, the squeezing of the face and all that doesn't even look pleasurable! It looks rather painful! Don't get me wrong, I'm not saying that there is anything wrong with this kind of orgasm, but it's only one experience out of a vast range of possibilities.

The release of the peak orgasm is a way to throw off energy and on a subconscious level, it goes hand in hand with shame. The sexual energy is so wild and so intense, and if we haven't done the healing work, unconsciously we tend to rush into releasing this intensity.

Energetic, etheric or tantric orgasm is a totally different story.

We are not trying to arrive anywhere or get rid of anything. On the contrary, we consciously let the energy build and spread throughout our body, and possibly even beyond.

Yes, it does take energetic awareness — and it is not very difficult to develop. It entails a willingness to play bigger, to step up in our human experience.

My invitation is to acknowledge even the slightest sensation of pleasure in the body as orgasmic. We need to learn to feel pleasure. We have a long history of feeling unworthy of joy without any reason. We may even call it shallow. Many also have a deep unconscious belief that we need to struggle to succeed. It is ingrained in our field of consciousness, but on top of that, many have had traumatic experiences that have left a deep imprint of guilt. This is the reason why we are so disconnected from natural pleasure that is in fact accessible to us at all times.

Try it now...

Wherever you are, if you are sitting down, feel the sensation in your thighs and bum touching the surface of the chair. Move a little, give yourself a little more space, relax your pelvic floor. Doesn't it feel nice?

Feel the air touching your cheek. Can you feel the pleasure of it? This is a tiny orgasm! Yes, you are experiencing it now!

Now include breath and movement. Unclench your body,
relax your jaw, feel into the sensation a bit more…

It's not that you need to produce any specific circumstances for orgasm to take place. Just allow what is here now. Life is full of pleasure. We need to start seeing that, because this alone creates a powerful shift of a disempowering paradigm.

Orgasm is an experience of full connectedness with Life. It is when we are feeling fully alive. And Life shifts, Life moves, and we are designed to move with it, with all of it!

Our emotions are also an expression of Life. When we dare to fully feel them, we start fully feeling Life.

A fully lived emotion is an orgasm.

Have you ever experienced an orgasm through rage? When fully lived, no emotion lasts. There is so much beauty to each and every one. What it gives us is a full experience of life. And this is orgasmic.

Here is a description of an orgasm by yours truly:

The wildest celebration of life

At times quiet
At times growling
At times roaring
At times begging for some love

29

Liberation into Orgasm

At times weeping
At times crying the eyes out
At times embodying the predator
At times embodying the prey
And after all there is no victim

Prey longs for the predator
Prey longs to surrender

And always wild WILD WILD
Wildness is our natural state
Wildness is freedom

Life I celebrate You
Life I celebrate Me
Life I celebrate

Life fully lived is Orgasm
Orgasm is what happens when we fully live this Life

And all that… is painted on the canvas of serenity.
As serenity is the true nature of God.

5
Typology of Orgasms

We can separate orgasms into two large categories: physical orgasms and energetic orgasms.

Physical or Grasping Orgasms

Physical orgasm is the peak pleasure that we experience as result of physical stimulation. After intense experience in the body, in some cases, pleasure can move up from the genitals and spread through the body.

We can classify those orgasms into several categories, but in reality, they all may be happening at the same time.

Physical Orgasms for women:
- Clitoral orgasm
- G-spot orgasm
- Vaginal orgasm
- Cervical (cervico-uterine) orgasm
- Anal orgasm

- Breast orgasm
- Throat orgasm

Physical Orgasms for men:
- Ejaculatory orgasm
- Multi-ejaculatory orgasm
- Retrograde ejaculatory (Million-dollar point) orgasm
- Physical orgasm without ejaculation
- Anal orgasm (prostatic)
- Prostatic orgasm with ejaculation
- Nipple orgasm
- Mouth orgasm
- Throat-gasm

Energetic, Etheric or Full-Body Orgasm

Energetic orgasm is an orgasm that happens primarily in our energetic body. The energetic body surrounds the physical just like a glove, and permeates it as well.

How to move from only genital-driven pleasure to full-body orgasmic experiences?

A huge difference between physical orgasm and energetic full-body orgasm is that in physical orgasm we are grasping for pleasure, when in the energetic orgasm we let go into complete surrender. This becomes a really profound spiritual experience.

Yes, there is a way to have an orgasm with the whole body.

Yes, there is a way to feel that our orgasm is a portal into infinity.

Yes, orgasmic freedom will create freedom in all aspects of your life.

First we need to understand the teachings of the Five Bodies of a Human Being. This knowledge hails from yoga and from western esoteric traditions. It also has been partly studied scientifically. I will be going into this teaching in detail below.

6
Types of Orgasm for Women

Now we will go on a journey into orgasmic country. There will be peaks and valleys. Enjoy the ride!

1. Clitoral orgasm

It is an orgasm that happens in the clitoris, in most cases caused by its stimulation. The intensity of sensation builds against pressure and this orgasm happens as a release of the intensity. It is quick and electric. Usually, it comes together with an energetic explosion.

For most women it's the easiest orgasm. For many, it's the only one they have ever acknowledged or experienced.

Usually this type of orgasm explodes very quickly and causes a discharge of energy. Right after the orgasm, the clitoris becomes extremely sensitive. The woman doesn't want to be touched for some time. This is actually a sign that some energy was lost. Then comes a refractory period, for some women it is very quick — just a couple of minutes, when for others it may be up to 24 hours.

In some tantric schools, clitoral orgasm has a bad reputation because of the loss of energy. What is more disturbing, in my point of view, is that this might result in an energetic dip or (even if short) disconnection.

> *I made an experiment during which for a duration of a month I was bringing myself to clitoral orgasms nearly every day. About a week into this experiment I started having lower back pains. I was feeling more emotional that usually, my period was much heavier than normally. Even though I had fun having quick, intense and easy pleasure, by the end of the month I felt rather depleted.*

2. Orgasm from vaginal opening

This is the orgasm that happens at the level of the ring of muscles just at the entrance of the yoni (vagina). It usually happens when the lingam (penis) is rhythmically going in and out of the yoni.

This orgasm usually comes with a deep urge for pounding and wanting to be filled. This orgasm can be imploded and channeled upwards, which will activate the kundalini — raw sexual energy often represented by a symbol of a snake coiled at the level of the woman's root chakra.

3. Orgasms that come from the vaginal walls and the G-spot orgasm

When a woman's yoni is open, she is highly sensitive to pleasure. An orgasm can happen from the walls of the vagina, or from a specific area called the G-spot.

The name is associated with a scientist who proved the existence of the G-spot — Dr. Ernst Gräfenberg. This is where we see that sometimes the science is behind our understanding. By the time of its discovery, many women had already known of the existence of the G-spot from direct experience. That's why I say it's better to refer to the G-spot as the Goddess spot, not the Gräfenberg spot.

It is also not necessarily a "spot", but an area that begins about four centimeters inside the yoni, on the frontal wall. When a woman is aroused this tissue begins to swell. In the structure of the G-spot there is erectile tissue. Before the actual orgasm, the woman might experience a sensation that she needs to pee. Yet, it is a terrible time to run to the bathroom!

After experiencing and "being fluent" at this kind of orgasm, women never want to go back to clitoral orgasm.

This orgasm can come together with female ejaculation or amrita. More on that soon in chapter "Amrita".

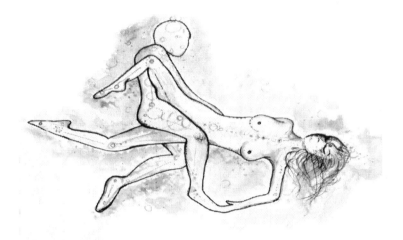

A great position for cervical stimulation

4. Cervical or cervico-uterine orgasm

This is a very powerful and important form of orgasm as it has the potential to produce highly spiritual effects. Cervico-uterine orgasm is definitely a mystical experience.

The cervix is the neck of the uterus, which is an incredibly magical organ. This kind of orgasm arises from inside the womb. Waves of pleasure happen inside of the womb, from there very easily they are transformed into waves of pleasure spreading through the entire body. The energy spreads and activates all energetic centers automatically. Very often it comes along with a strong arousal of kundalini and it results in a whole-body orgasm. For some women, it brings a strong activation of the third chakra, the manipura chakra, and the sensation is as if belly is on fire.

All sorts of mystical experiences can happen with this type of orgasm — the woman may stop breathing, she may change personality — all of a sudden a timid woman may start growling like a tiger, tears might start streaming down her face. A woman can experience a higher state of consciousness. It is also very common that a woman experiences a big opening of the heart, as there is an energetic channel that runs from the cervix to the heart. On top of that, this orgasm comes with a lot of pleasure.

A note on hard pounding:

Since the cervix is located quite deep inside of the yoni, you may think that in order to experience cervical stimulation, the woman needs to be taken really hard. However, hard pounding should take place in only one case: when the woman is highly, utterly and absolutely aroused. In any other case, this is a no go and, in some cases, it can cause the uterus to become displaced. It's not the end of the world, it can be placed into the right position with some forms of healing massage, but most women don't even know that their uterus is displaced. Besides some physiological disturbance, it also can give a woman a sense that she is out of her center.

A woman's uterus is not a fixed organ. It moves depending on two factors:
1. where she is in her cycle,
2. what her arousal level is.

Nature has created us in such a smart way, that when we are most aroused, the uterus lifts up and therefore, the cervix is located higher in the vagina.

We are designed in this way so that in case of ejaculation, the sperm can stay in the vaginal canal longer and therefore, chances for procreation are higher.

What is interesting for our "research" here is that in this case the yoni is more open, there is plenty of natural lubrication, the cervix is higher up and this is when we can go wild, if we choose to do so.

The cervix is a very sensitive area. Usually when you only start exploring the cervix, it is either very painful or numb. Very often, energy in this area is blocked. Normally, it is not touched during lovemaking because it is too intense for the woman. Or, it is stimulated, but the woman does not feel anything because to escape from the intensity she developed numbness.

A great position for cervical stimulation

Cervical orgasm is the only form of orgasm for which size matters. If there is a big mismatch in the length of man's lingam and a woman's yoni, this area will never be touched. Although there are several positions that can help. But a man who is deeply in touch with his lingam can energetically fill a woman.

5. Anal

This orgasm requires anal penetration. Anal stimulation or sex is highly recommended for people who have a strong tendency for control and for people who have very heavy energy.

Before actual penetration, you need to make sure that the woman is deeply relaxed. It is best to move into anal stimulation after a good session of vaginal penetration. In any case, it is good to start with a massage of the bum, sacrum and anus. Make sure to use a lot of oil or lubricant. And very important-ly — take plenty of time. For some women, massage is already enough to go into anal orgasm and liberate a lot of energy.

Normally, anal sex is an incredibly powerful experience be-cause it takes a lot of vulnerability to do it. The anal orgasm is a very unique sensation and incredibly powerful! It may come together with a clitoral orgasm.

If you want some guidance for your anal play, I included a whole chapter on it.

6. Throat-gasm

Ok, this might be pushing your comfort zone, but why stay comfortable when Life has so much to offer if we dare to open up?

Throat orgasm is a mystical experience that may occur as result of deep throating. The woman performs a blow job on the man, and she takes his lingam very deep into the throat.

Through this practice, the lingam will press against a secret reflexology point deep inside her throat, which may induce a state of spiritual trance and other paranormal happenings.

Deep throating also stimulates the vagus nerve, which goes through all of our organs.
It opens us in such a way that it naturally lifts away all limitations of the natural expression of our sexual self.

Through deep throating, a woman can produce a mystical secretion that is called throat ejaculation. In tantric texts, it is said that this liquid is called soma or the sacred nectar, secreted from the soma chakra located on the back of the head. It is not saliva. This is obvious because saliva doesn't come in such amounts.

To receive a lingam really deep in your throat the woman needs to go past the gag reflex. It is best to do it on an empty stomach.

7. Breast-gasm

Breast-gasm is another fascinating type of orgasm for women.

Our breasts have a yang quality to them. They are very visible, even if covered by layers of clothing. From an early age, we all have been getting messages from the media about the ideal breast size, the ideal breast shape. If we feel we don't measure up, we start to disconnect from our breasts.

Some women even physically cut open their breasts and enlarge them with implants to fit into the societally accepted version of an ideal female body.

Once we disconnect from our breasts, they simply go numb.

When in their natural state, our breasts are our love center as they sit on either side of our spiritual heart or anahata chakra. Our breasts are actually the physical extension of our heart. They represent the external expression of our heart energy. Also, they are sensual and orgasmic.

In the ancient Taoist tradition, breasts are seen as the feminine plus pole. Natural feminine radiance and power comes from our heart area. We actually penetrate the world with our breasts and we can penetrate our partner and the whole world with our love.

Our breasts are closely connected to our yoni and when they are stimulated, the same area of the brain gets activated. Stimulating, massaging and caressing the breasts also helps us open our hearts and feel connected. We sensitize our breasts by doing breast massage and we train ourselves for breast-gasms.

42

My call to all women: Burn your bra!

Ok, don't burn the La Perla, but only use it for special occasions, for a few hours a week if you want.

There was a study that concluded that breasts gain no support or benefit from being supported by a bra. Wearing a bra means that the supporting tissues will not grow and they will wither, causing the breasts to degrade over time. This might be surprising, but it's about time to question things that we've been so accustomed to, because — let's face it — neither the media, nor bra-producing companies could care less about our health. Also, those who wear bras 18 – 24 hours a day have a 100 times greater incidence of breast cancer than those who choose not to wear one.

Breasts are meant to move as you walk around, and that movement will keep the lymph moving and breasts healthy. Tight bras and metal underwire are an even bigger issue — they completely block the lymph and energy flow around your breasts and heart center. Intense push-ups do the same.

If you are having a sexy date and only wear your bra for a couple of hours (or minutes) before it gets taken off — go for it! But seriously don't wear tight and compressing bras on a daily basis. Yoga tops can be very tight too. There are non-compressing bra-tops, which are made in pretty lace or sometimes can be found in natural fabric. I personally love these.

Breast Massage, Why?

Massaging out breasts regularly helps to harmonize our hormones, fills our breasts with energy and allows us to own this beautiful part of our bodies and open our hearts. It also helps move the blood and the lymph and prevents the formation of lumps, and therefore, prevents breast cancer. Our breasts mainly consist of fat tissue. Fat tends to store a lot of toxins. As we massage our breasts, we release lots of toxins.

It's great for women to learn the techniques of great massage and massage their breasts regularly, and also it is great to offer breast massage to your partner. You may be uncomfortable at first with touching your own breasts. Believe me, it doesn't take long for women to get into this practice. My students have shared with me the effects they feel from breast massage. They said this practice makes them feel nurtured, calm, aroused, beautiful and loving.

Breast massage is a wonderful start to the day. Sometimes, I do it even before I get up. I keep a bottle of coconut oil next to my bed, and on some mornings I spread it over my breasts, add a couple of drops of a delicious essential oil and offer myself a nurturing experience of breast massage. Rose oil is especially great because it has the vibration of our heart chakra and helps harmonize energy in this area. Pomegranate oil is another great essential oil to use for our precious breasts.
Evenings work wonderfully too. I find that breast massage performed in the evenings helps release the stress of the day.

By all means, do breast massage as soon as you take off your bra on the days when you choose to wear it.

How do I massage my breasts?

Warm your hands by rubbing them together vigorously. Take some oil. Place your hands on your breasts, and begin to gently rub inwards using a circular motion (see the image below). This means your right hand will be moving clockwise, while your left hand moves counter-clockwise. Each rub should last a couple of seconds. Continue for as long as you like. Lightly trace the skin in circular motions with the nipples at the center of the circle. Do not hold the breasts and move them — skim the surface of the skin. If you are receiving breast massage — enjoy the sensations and connect with the warm pleasurable feelings. Alternate between light and firm touch. Feel free to improvise, maybe you will come up with some techniques of your own. Just do what feels juicy and delightful.

What about the nipples?

Massaging the nipples activates our endocrine system and aids in the production of lubrication in our yoni. So take time to play with the nipples. Try lightly squeezing them and gently twisting. As women practice daily breast massage, they notice that they begin to inhabit their breasts more.

The breasts respond to touch differently: they become more sensitive, they may grow and become more firm.

Stimulation for breast-gasms

If you want to go on the sacred journey with your lover called Breast-gasms, follow these steps. Give it at least 20 minutes or more.

•   First you want to receive consent. You can ask something like: *"Would you like me to perform a ritual in honor and adoration of your delectable breasts?"*
•   Begin by massaging the breasts with your hands and alternate between firm and very light touch. Go slowly and stay very present.
•   Do not touch the nipples just yet.
•   Keep on stimulating her breasts in the most creative ways and do not stop. You can use your hands like brushes that cover each and every millimeter of the skin. She might feel ticklish or get nervous, or she may start laughing, crying or moving like a fish on the sand. Stay present and do not stop, no matter what.
•   Start stimulating the whole breast with your tongue.
•   When she is very hot, gradually start making your

46

way to the nipple. Tease her. Keep building tension. You are approaching the nipple like you would be approaching the yoni — only start touching it when she is yearning for it!

•   Lightly touch the nipples with the middle of your palm. Then try licking them and stimulating them with each side of your tongue. This will produce different sensations.

•   Lightly squeeze the nipples. Alternate between stimulating her with your hands, lips and mouth. Suck on the nipples. Breathe on the nipples.

•   Follow the flow, keep building the intensity, and encourage her to open to the sensations, even if it feels uncomfortable and tickles.

•   Once she is highly aroused — just keep doing what you are doing. *When her pleasure is very high, sometimes liquid may be secreted from the nipples. This liquid is super potent and has mystical and healing properties.*

After 20 minutes of such play, the pleasure hormones, the endorphins, kick in and she is very likely to experience a breastgasm. Don't be discouraged if she reaches a plateau. Many women's breasts need to go through a process of sensitizing before they can actually orgasm. With such play, you are waking up neural pathways, which means that the breasts get more and more orgasmic.

> *I lay on my back and he is playing with my breasts. He is taking plenty of time and offering me his full presence. I keep my awareness in my breasts. His touch is guiding me deeper and deeper into the sensation. At times, he barely touches my skin. At times, he squeezes my nipples. At times, he squeezes my entire breasts and shakes them wildly. This sends shivers all through my body. It's been a good 20 minutes and the waves of pleasure are only*

47

building. Suddenly, I am taken by my own laughter. I feel bubbles of energy spreading through my chest. It feels like colorful fireworks shooting from my very heart. It is joyful. It feels like a celebration. Oh yes, it is a celebration. And, I want the world to celebrate with me.

7
Men's Role in Female Orgasm

When it comes to sex, the default mode for most men is performance. Men deeply want to be the hero for their partners. Usually, this translates to wanting to please and due to the lack of sexual education that we have, in our minds to please means to impress.

It may surprise you, but in most situations the best thing a man can do is just be there and not even move.
Men need to shift their focus from performance to presence. What women really need for expansion both in sex and in life is your presence. Men just need to show up. Drop the idea that you need to move in a certain way, pound her and "give it to her."

Women have to stop believing that she gets her orgasms from the man. Orgasms are yours and you are the one that takes yourself to the place to experience them. Opening to your own energy — that's pretty much all it takes. It is all about cultivating presence, for both partners.

49

What a man can do for for a woman is hold the container for her experience to unfold. Be there, unintimidated by anything, but offering his full heart, supporting his partner's unfolding and encouraging her to keep opening.

I could teach you all sorts of very complex techniques. Yet, the ability to perform those is not what makes you advanced. What makes you advanced is your capacity to be present. When you can really be in the experience, don't be seduced by your own thoughts — then the most simple things can open you up and blow your mind.

> *One of the most powerful experiences I had in sex was when my partner was inside me all through the night. Eight hours straight. He was inside and we would fall asleep. Then, half-asleep half-awake., enjoying the closeness to him, I would moan quietly and move my hips a little. That would re-activate the flow of orgasmic energy. Then, I would come to stillness again and fall into sleep. Then he would wake up, squeeze me tighter, make a couple of soft movements, and fall asleep again.*

8
Types of Orgasm for Men

Male orgasm is far more complex than what we normally believe. Men can also experience physical and energetic orgasms.

Let's start with the physical ones. Just like women, male physical orgasms can either begin and end at the level of genitals, or they can spread through the whole body and develop into a full-body experience.

Varieties of Physical Orgasms for Men:
- Ejaculatory orgasm
- Multi-ejaculatory orgasm
- Retrograde ejaculatory (Million-dollar point) orgasm
- Physical orgasm without ejaculation
- Anal orgasm (prostatic)
- Prostatic orgasm with ejaculation
- Nipple orgasm
- Mouth orgasm
- Throat-gasm

Most men find it very surprising when they first find out that they can have an orgasm without ejaculation. Yes, it is a learnable skill.

When men teach themselves to disassociate orgasm and ejaculation, it enhances dramatically their experience of orgasmic energy. It may feel very subtle at first: the man will notice a tingling, a shiver or a warm sensation. The heart rate and breathing may change. It is an orgasm but it is not the kind of orgasm that men are used to.

First, let's look at different types of physical orgasms.

1. Ejaculatory orgasm

Ejaculatory orgasm is characterized by a quick and intense sensation in the penis. Ejaculation is a series of contractions that comes together with discharge of semen which constitutes of lubrication and (usually) sperm. This is what all men are familiar with and most believe that this is the only way for them to orgasm. It's interesting though that many men report that in their early phase of life, when they were only starting to connect with their sexuality, they could not achieve ejaculation. They could last very long without any need to ejaculate. It made many of them feel inadequate, due to the type of sexuality that porn presents or, perhaps, because of the dissatisfaction of their partner (who, of course, was also conditioned by porn.)

2. Multi-ejaculatory orgasm

These orgasms are quite rare. Yet, some men with very strong
vitality can experience multi-ejaculatory orgasms meaning that
they can maintain an erection and ejaculate in waves, several
times in a row.

3. Retrograde ejaculatory (Million-dollar point) orgasm

In this case, the man will be prolonging the act of lovemaking,
staying at about 60-70% of pleasure. Then he will feel that
ejaculation is approaching, the contractions may have already
started, and he will pull out his lingam and as quickly as
possible and as strongly as possible press on his perineum with
three fingers. This will stop the ejaculation from coming out,
but may cause something that's called "injaculation" — the
ejaculate will stay in the canal, and might even go into the
bladder. I do not recommend this method.

4. Physical orgasm without ejaculation

This refers to the sharp sensations of the ejaculatory orgasm
that most men are used to, but the actual liquid won't come out
of the penis.
Usually this orgasm will spread throughout the whole body
(see the chapter on energetic orgasms), but it does take
willingness and awareness to go into it fully.

5. Anal orgasm (prostatic)

It is incredibly powerful for men to experience being penetrated. It opens up an incredibly vulnerable inner space. Many men never allow themselves to be vulnerable because of the silent taboo of society. Society tells us that men need to be strong and they can never cry. This results in a big suppression of emotions. When we suppress emotions, the energy cannot flow. Therefore, we are also blocking our orgasmic potential.

Experiencing prostate stimulation is an amazing way of regaining the capacity for vulnerability and also accessing the feminine side. It is so beautiful to witness a man opening up to experiencing his soft and vulnerable side. In no way does it makes him less of a man. It definitely makes him a larger human being.

This practice brings many benefits including stronger erections, deeper orgasms, the prevention of prostate disease and the release of shame and sexual trauma.

To activate the prostate, it is great to perform a massage, during which first the lingam and the whole body will be activated. Then, very gently the anus will be massaged, both externally and if he is ready for it — internally.

Where is the prostate?

The prostate is a gland that is said to be the male version of the G-spot.

It is a **walnut-sized gland** located between the bladder and the penis. The prostate is just in front of the rectum. It is located on the frontal wall of the anus (the side of the penis), about three – four inches (seven – ten centimeters) away. It feels like a nickel.

The recommended position for prostate massage is when the man is laying on his back.
Stimulation of the prostate can create incredible orgasms for men. It is called "prostate milking," and you can do it either by yourself or receive it from your partner.

How to massage the prostate?

Tap it, stroke it forward and back, or side to side, caress it in a clockwise or counterclockwise fashion.
Keep reminding your partner to breathe into the sensation. Some men experience orgasm from the first session of anal massage, for others it takes more time. This kind of orgasm can be incredibly intense. It may feel like a complete letting go into the unknown, and it may easily move into a full-body orgasm.

6. Anal orgasm with ejaculation

Sometimes an anal orgasm comes together with ejaculation.

7. Nipple orgasm

Some men naturally have incredibly sensitive nipples, others can develop their sensitivity over time. Orgasms that are brought on by nipple stimulation can also occur. For this to happen, the man needs to open into the sensation of tingling, open into the sensitivity as his partner continuously stimulates the nipple with the tongue, teeth, lips and fingers.

8. Mouth orgasm

This type of orgasm may occur when a man is performing the oral stimulation of a yoni (cunnilingus).

If you allow yourself to really enjoy the sensation of your tongue against the yoni of a woman, you may experience an explosion of excitement in your mouth!

It may feel like your mouth is being energetically coated by stardust.

9. Throat-gasms

Throat-gasms are totally available to men as well, and not only for homosexual men. You can stimulate the back of the man's throat with the fingers or dildo. Just as with a woman, the man needs to open beyond the gag reflex, relax through the sensations and let the magic happen.

A helpful tip: as you feel the gag reflex, try doing a few swallowing motions.

Ejaculation mastery

Any man can learn to be fully in control of his ejaculation, and ejaculate only when he chooses to do so.

Most people equate male orgasm with ejaculation. In fact, orgasm and ejaculation are two different things. As explained in the previous chapter, men are capable of experiencing very deep orgasms without ejaculation whatsoever.

Ejaculation mastery – What is it?

Ejaculation mastery is an ancient Taoist and tantric practice, which is referred to preservation of the seed and the vital force, what is known as the chi or prana.

When you have mastery over your ejaculation you have the choice of when you want to ejaculate as opposed to ejaculating compulsively, which is the case for most men in this world.

Once you have mastered your ejaculation, you may make love for as long as you like and you may choose whether you want to ejaculate in the end or not. If you do choose to ejaculate because your intuition tells you so, you can make a little ritual out of it.

One tablespoon of semen is incredibly powerful stuff.
In addition to sperm cells, seminal fluid contains immense amounts of protein, vitamins, minerals and amino acids as well as vital energies.

In ancient Chinese medicine, semen was viewed as life-force energy.

Semen contained in a man's body represents tremendous individual potential and creative power. It should be viewed as a type of liquid gold, and treated as sacred.

It is believed that every time a man ejaculates, he drains his vital power. Therefore, if a man ejaculates too frequently he suffers detrimental effects to his health. This becomes especially apparent after the 40s. The effects may include a lack of vitality, and even impotence.

The vast majority of men will admit that after an ejaculation they feel depleted, low in energy, disconnected and/or withdrawn.

Containment of semen will empower a man because the vital substance nourishes his intelligence and creativity. He becomes more centered and a master of himself.

A healthy adult male can release between 40 million and 1.2 billion sperm cells in a single ejaculation. Each sperm cell is a seed of Life. In Tantra, we view Life as something that is incredibly sacred. *So when a man chooses to cultivate his sexual energy and not spill his seed, he makes the choice to contain the sacredness of Life.*

Besides health benefits, which Taoism teaches us about, there are also numerous other benefits of ejaculatory mastery, such as:

- prolonging the duration of lovemaking,
- cultivating greater desire and connectedness with your partner,
- elimination of a refractory period (loss of energy after ejaculation), so you can make love again and again at any time,
- the ability to experience and cultivate deeper full-body orgasms,
- facilitating deep orgasms for your female partner (women need anywhere between 20 to 40 minutes of lovemaking before they can actually drop into very deep orgasmic states),
- greater health and vitality,
- increased power in all areas of your life,
- helping shift the mentality of goal-oriented sex.

Ejaculation mastery takes a lot of will, dedication and patience. Men who are mastering ejaculation are not only rewriting deeply-rooted neurological patterns, but also changing the frequency at which their energy vibrates, making it more and more refined. You can imagine that this alone has a huge effect on the entire life of a man, including his business, relationships and all other areas of his life.

It may surprise you, but women play a very big role in men's desire to ejaculate.

The desire to get a man to ejaculate is very strong because of nature's programming. It's the way we have been programmed so we can survive as a species.

What makes a man ejaculate is the pull of Shakti. This pull comes from nature itself. It comes from the never-ending desire of Life for Life.

This is something that needs to be recognized. Once it is — it is easier to separate yourself from it.

As long as ejaculation happens automatically, you are being entirely controlled by nature. Each man is biologically programmed: nature wants him to impregnate as many females as possible, so that Life can go on!

When you follow the agenda of nature, you don't fully own a big part of your consciousness — your will. On our path to awakening, we are always aiming to overcome what is mechanical and automatic in our nature and replace it by an act of will.

When men first hear about ejaculation control some have this question: "Do you mean I am not supposed to orgasm?" The answer is no, it doesn't mean that.

> *Once I was with a lover who told me from the start: "I love sex and I think I'm pretty good at it, but I want you to guide me so we can do it the tantric way."*
> *We were making love and it was exquisite, and after quite a long time he asked me: "Can I cum now?"*
> *I said: "Yes, but do not ejaculate".*
> *He asked: "Are you sure it's possible?"*
> *"Yes," I said, "100% sure."*
> *He seemed surprised for a second, but then something amazing happened. He had an orgasm! And he did not ejaculate.*
> *So all it took for him was being in the highly-aroused state and me telling him that he could separate orgasm and ejaculation. He trusted me and let the experience unfold.*

The flow of semen only contributes to orgasm but does not create it.

How to master ejaculation?

There are numerous yogic techniques that can help and I won't go into detail here, but here are five main keys to ejaculation mastery:

• Understanding the scale of pleasure
• Breath
• Relaxation and "dropping" into your pelvis and your genitals
• Sublimation
• Practice

1. Understand where you are on the scale of pleasure

0 - non arousal
10 - full-blown orgasm

As you build pleasure when self-pleasuring or during intercourse, be very conscious of what number you are on the arousal scale. When you get to six or seven out of ten — don't start thinking about your grandmother, but pause, breathe deeply and be still. You are close to the edge, but you are not going to tip over it. Then find a way to stay on this level. Pause as often as you need, you may even pull out and do some exercises (literally, do push ups, jump up and down a few times) — this will help you move the energy.

A supportive partner is gold!

With practice your edge will extend, and you will notice that you can stay at seven and a half and even eight for prolonged periods of time.

2. When approaching orgasm the breath naturally becomes very fast and shallow. This is exactly the opposite of what you need to do. Breathe deeply and steadily — especially when you are at seven. Take three deep breaths, inhale for four counts and exhale for four counts.

3. I am a big advocate of the importance of relaxing into and owning our genitals.
Social conditioning and shame are the reasons for our major disconnect from our genitals, and therefore — our power.

Men accumulate stress and tension in their genitals, and put themselves under incredible performance pressure. There may be fear of not being good enough, fear of coming too soon, trying to be the best lover for his woman. All this causes habitual tension in the pelvic floor. All those fears originate in one place: a **goal-oriented mentality.** It is as if we have an image in our minds about what "good sex" means. This places an incredible amount of pressure on people because if we are fixed on achieving that goal of "good sex" and if we think that we don't measure up, we tense up.

Plus, working toward building to a climax literally prevents us from the fullness of the experience, from being rooted in the present moment, and offering that presence to our partner.

It takes a lot of de-conditioning. Often our desire to have an orgasm is why most of us want sex. But this is an invitation to let go of any kind of goal. If you want to experience what the true potential of sex is, dare to shift your attitude.

It is also tricky because what we inherit from society is that simply relaxing into the space of being and non-doing, we judge as laziness or lack of ambition. Goal-oriented culture does not approve of that. As I said before — modern life is the killer of pleasure. We really need to put our will into reclaiming our birthright, which are those full orgasms.

Learn to give space to your genitals. Bring your awareness into your genitals and feel the gravity of the Earth. Relax your entire body. Your penis and your testicles have to become the place of anchoring, the place where you can tune in any time and feel planted and grounded in your power. You also need to give yourself the permission to feel the pleasure that comes together with that relaxation.

A simple practice to try: *from time to time throughout the day scan your body and consciously relax any places of tension.*

To master ejaculation the best thing a man can do is slow down, or even stop, relax back into his body and take several deep breaths. This will take the focus off increasing the excitement and help to bring more attention to the body in the present moment.

63

Drop the goal. As soon as the goal of sex is dropped, relaxation into the present follows naturally.

4. Sublimation is a tantric term and "Upward Draw" is a Taoist term, the techniques are slightly different, but basically what both are doing is they are moving your energy from heavier energetic centers to lighter energetic centers, that is from the lower chakras to the higher chakras.

As you bring your attention to your genitals and as you approach the point of no return — slow down, breathe and visualize that the energy is moving from your pelvis upwards to your heart and all the way to the top of the head.

Normally, when we come into a peak state of arousal, the seed moves out horizontally, to procreate. The yogic, tantric and Taoist view shows us that there is a way to redirect the energy vertically up the spine.

5. To master ejaculation you need to practice, both by practicing self-pleasuring (preferably, daily) and by having tantric sex.
Just like lovemaking, tantric self pleasure looks very different to "jerking off". The main difference is that you don't have a goal. No goal of arriving to a peak experience. You are self pleasuring for the sake of enjoying your own beauty and eroticism.

9
Woman's Role in Male Orgasm

There are two parts to this one.

1. If you want to practice the sacred sexuality and Tantra together with your partner, you need to commit to becoming a team or even better — consorts. In this way, you won't only focus on your needs, agendas and projection regarding what your partner may want. In this configuration, you actually choose to commit to expand together beyond your personalities, focus on the big picture of what really is available for you as a couple, whether you have a life ahead together or just an hour.

Have you ever felt into the might of the ocean? Or the power of a thunderstorm? Can you imagine how much intensity there is when a volcano is erupting?

It is magnificent and this force is incredibly intense. Actually, you don't need to go on an expedition to witness it because that same force resides right there in your genitals. Another name for this force is Shakti.

Shakti is the Sanskrit name for energy, power and the entire manifested world. It is the counterpart to Shiva — unborn awareness.

Some aspects of our life are charged with a particularly strong Shakti. Sexuality has a very strong Shakti. When the Shakti is that strong it's really hard to control it. Imagine trying to control the ocean. It is from the realms of the superpowers and yet Tantra proves that it is possible to control our sexual energy.

What makes a man ejaculate is the pull of Shakti. This pull is coming from nature itself. From the never-ending desire of Life for Life. When he ejaculates, he misses the opportunity to cultivate those bigger, more expansive orgasms.

This is to give you a picture what men are dealing with.

Life needs to go on, and for that, we need to procreate. It is completely natural to have a pull and desire to conceive a baby. For this, nature has given us intercourse. However, humans discovered that sex doesn't have to always lead to conception. It can be a very pleasant and life-enriching expression of love. It can help us feel very intimate with our loved one and some even approach it as a spiritual practice.

Coming back to the power of volcano — even if we have consciously decided that we are not using sex to make babies, Shakti, nature, is not going anywhere. Nature has her own agenda — it wants you to procreate. It can actually be very tricky — around a certain age many women feel a strong desire to have babies. It might be hard to distinguish if it is a pull of nature or if it's your conscious decision.

This pull of nature is especially strong when we are making love. This pull is exactly what makes a man ejaculate. This pull is exactly what makes a woman want to be filled with her lover's sperm. Very often, this happens completely unconsciously. You may feel that at certain points, especially when the pleasure is intense, you just want to drink him, suck him in, feel all of him inside you. This moment is very, very crucial.

If you become aware of this instinct and how it manifests at the level of your energetic and emotional bodies, you can learn to master your sexual energy and **even help your man last longer.**

Your pull, your Shakti, is a major component to his ejaculation.

If you want him to last longer, you need to realize that you are the main component.

The moment when you want to suck him in so much, and desire is so intense, is exactly the moment when you are pulling his energy inside of you and that's when he is very likely to ejaculate. If in this moment you stop the pull, relax the energetic grip, you help him tremendously to prolong intercourse.

It may sound very complicated, and yes, it is a subtle thing that you do with your energy. Once you get a hold of it, however, it will become completely natural for you. Therefore, the man will be able to last longer and your chance of experiencing those big orgasms is infinitely higher.

This kind of help goes way beyond opening to better orgasms. When we are holding each other with our presence, we are supporting each other's evolution and therefore, **our unfolding into the most expanded version of ourselves.** I don't know of a greater service than that.

2. Woman's role in a man's orgasm cannot be underestimated, as the strongest orgasms a man can experience are powered and facilitated by the feminine.

It is identical in the case of a homosexual couple — the partner who is more in touch with his feminine carries more Shakti. You should know by now that in Tantra we love Shakti, we love energy, any kind of energy, because the more energy — the stronger the orgasms, the bigger states of consciousness that we can experience, the more power we give to our kundalini.

A woman can consciously open her energetic field to the man, invite him in, hold back nothing, receive him into her womb, hold him and take him on a journey with her.

It takes willingness from a man to surrender to the Shakti of his woman, and let himself go on this journey.

As she goes into an orgasm, the man can tune into her and let himself go into her waves of pleasure.

10
Full-Body Orgasm

Other names for full-body orgasm are energetic, etheric, multi- or tantric orgasm.

How do we move from only genital-driven pleasure to full-body orgasmic experiences?

A huge difference between a physical orgasm and an energetic full-body orgasm is that in physical orgasm we are grasping for pleasure, when in the energetic orgasm we let go into complete surrender. The latter becomes a profound spiritual experience.

Yes, there is a way to have an orgasm with the whole body — and even beyond the body.

Deep orgasms take a lot of vulnerability and may feel incredibly revealing. You may even start crying spontaneously, without any story going on in your head. This is very beautiful. It is always a sign of opening.

Our job is to surrender and be washed by the waves of orgasm. Most people cut off from their experience because they are bombarded by unconscious fears or even a sense of unworthiness, a voice in their head that is saying: *"Can I really have that much pleasure?"*

Full-body orgasms are accessible to everyone, yet men tend to suppress this experience more because in our culture men are "not supposed to" be expressive.

Before we dive any deeper, we need to understand the teachings of the Five Bodies of a Human Being. This knowledge hails from yoga, as well as from western esoteric traditions. It also has been partly studied scientifically.

The Five Bodies of a Human Being

According to the teaching of the Five Bodies of a Human Being, we consist not only of the physical body, that which we see every day in the mirror. In fact, it is just the tip of the iceberg. We are so much more.

1. The Physical Body is the one that is referred to in the you-are-what-you-eat type of sayings. Indeed, our physical body is nourished by the food we eat. Of course, whatever we do affects our energy too. The physical body is what is visible and tangible to all the parts of our make up.

2. The Energetic/Etheric Body permeates and surrounds the physical body. Sometimes it is referred to as the etheric double.

It has been studied by science, in fact, it can be measured, for example by means of Kirlian photography.

3. The Emotional/Astral Body is the body that houses our emotions.

4. The Mental Body is the level of our mind as well as our highest intelligence. The place that geniuses tap in.

5. The Causal Body, or the Body of Oneness, is the body of our Divine nature. The level of no level, where we are not separated from anything and anyone. This is the Body of Enlightenment.

What's interesting for our orgasmic "research" is our energetic or etheric body. It is possible for each and every human being to have an orgasm with the whole body. This kind of orgasm is also called tantric orgasm, multi orgasm or energetic orgasm.

It is called energetic orgasm because it is actually happening in your energetic body, which surrounds and permeates the body that you see every day in the mirror — the physical body.

Ways to train and strengthen the energetic body

Through sexuality and through energetic orgasms, we are training our energetic body.

There are many ways to strengthen the energetic body. Sports can be one of the ways. Compare a handshake with a person who does lots of sports and that of someone who hardly moves their body.

Of course, being athletic doesn't automatically mean that the person is orgasmic, but for these people, it's usually easier to open to their orgasmicness rather than for people who have not been taking care of their energy at all. A person who is sitting in front of TV or computer for 12 hours a day and eats junk food has a much weaker capacity.

Other ways to strengthen the energetic body is through dynamic energetic practices, yoga (especially hatha yoga), martial arts, chi gung, and other forms of energetic training.

Yet, I will say with utmost confidence, that tantric sexuality is the most efficient way to build your energetic body. I have done extensive research working with different people and investigating their etheric bodies, and I have found quite a dramatic difference between those who have regular powerful sexual experiences and those who don't.

It is not surprising for me, because when we are working with sexual energy we enter from the very basic energy, from the very core.

Through training, the energetic body becomes intelligent. Your energy actually becomes capable of "doing" things.

I'll name just a few things your energetic body can learn to do: move the energy throughout your body; feel what exactly is happening in the energetic body of your partner as if it was happening inside of you; feel someone else's pleasure; facilitate healing for oneself and others; facilitate better digestion; have an orgasm in any part of your body and many more things too.

72

The energetic body becomes alive and therefore, a much larger capacity for Life opens up to us. This is the body of Life. Life is pure energy. Shakti, as I mentioned before, the Sanskrit word used in Tantra to speak about the power, the feminine, the Goddess or Life, essentially means "energy". The more we are tapping into our own energy, the more we are tapping into Life.

The more Life becomes part of us and we become a part of Life, the more we actually become Life.

Keys to developing full body orgasms

There is a very central belief, especially when speaking about women, that it is our partners who give us orgasms. Although we can learn terrific skills for lovemaking, the idea that it is our partner who is responsible for our orgasm needs to shift, because it is a very disempowering belief. A belief that's coming from patriarchy. It is a mindset that is diminishing for us.

We don't have time to be disempowered.

So what I have to tell you is that it is entirely up to you whether you are going to have orgasms or not. A partner can open you up only to the degree that you are already open. The masterful partner is the one who is capable of holding space for that opening to reveal itself. "Ok, but how?" you may be wondering. "How do we get there?"

There are eight keys:

1.   Awareness

Awareness is your capacity to observe and witness yourself.

An orgasm is not going to happen if you are not there, if you are lost in your thoughts, plans or memories.

When we approach sexuality with awareness it transforms itself into a spiritual practice that creates love and deepens the experience of the present moment.

Awareness acts as a highly potent aphrodisiac too. Through awareness, we awaken to the body on an inner level and we actually notice how much pleasure there is in our life.

You are the one responsible for your life. You are the one responsible for your experience. You are the one responsible for your pleasure. You are the one who is in charge. You are the one who has to be present, to facilitate the background for your mind-blowing orgasm to unfold. Dropping in, opening, allowing.

See how you can make love with all of your body. Train yourself to be aware even of the slightest pleasure present in your body. See how you can experience pleasure in all of your body, offering it to pleasure, surrendering to it. Even now, wherever you are, you can soften some more. Liberate the spine, breathe a little deeper, drop into the pleasure that is already there. Just feeling your feet on the earth, bum on the chair or air touching your skin can be orgasmic. Even as we are breathing, it is highly sensual — we are making love — we are allowing the breath to enter us. All of it is your gateway to a deeper pleasure. I invite you to see even the slightest pleasure as an orgasm, even if a tiny little one.

Life is highly sensual and highly erotic. Only layers of shame are disconnecting us from it. In fact, these things are natural. They are real. They are accessible to each and every person.

2.   Breath

Many different breathing techniques exist, yet what is very simple and powerful is to just lengthen the breath. Try inhaling and exhaling for four counts. Breath is a great way to activate your life force. Relax your jaw and breathe through your mouth. With every inhalation, soften your body more and with every exhalation, relax deeper and let go. Breathe deeper and slower than you normally would.
With every inhalation, soften your body more and with every exhalation relax deeper and let go.

Whether you are practicing self-pleasure or are sensually or sexually connecting with your beloved, lengthen your breath. Normally, our breath is very shallow, but breath is the carrier of Life, so if we are not breathing fully, we are not allowing Life to fully reveal itself through us.

3.   Unclenched, relaxed body

Through habit and to one degree or another most of us are tense, clenched and disconnected from our body. Take a moment now to feel where the tension is in your body. Where do you clench your body due to habit? Now do the opposite — unclench. Give space to your belly. As you inhale bring your attention to your genitals and direct energy there.

We are taught to suck the belly in. Our belly is our emotional center, the center of our life force. Tight and clenched belly doesn't allow the energy and emotions to move freely. So here I invite you to drop into your body. Drop deeper and deeper through a "yes", through a continuous relaxation, through softening, saying yes to your belly and to all of Life.

This is something you can do moment by moment, all day. I encourage you to remember to do it especially during your sensual play or lovemaking.

Open to all sensations, allow them to really touch you. Fully experience what's happening. Keep dropping in, keep breathing deeply. Of course, this is only possible through presence. You cannot do any of this if your mind is busy with your to-do list or some other obsessive thoughts.

Make sure you relax your jaw, your belly and your pelvis.

I tell my students to do a body scan several times a day and relax all the clenched places. Eventually, it becomes a habit. It has numerous health benefits, including increase of blood flow to these areas and it is very important for us in our orgasmic cultivation.

4.   **Unclenched emotions = emotional flow**

We cannot be completely shut off in Life and then orgasm in

bed like crazy. Our emotions naturally want to flow, and that's what they do when we don't try to repress them. They change, shape-shift, get released, move and help us open up.
It is essential for our orgasmicness.

Notice what emotions are coming up for you, and instead of pushing them away, try allowing them. Allow them, even if it is one of the "uncomfortable" emotions, such as sadness, frustration or anger. You will see that when you actually feel your emotions, they tend to pass faster and flow.

Even the experience of being right in the midst of an emotion and staying with the emotional intensity can be a very orgasmic experience!

5. Sound

If you are not used to it, it might feel quite intimidating or uncomfortable to make sounds. You can begin by making a gentle "ha" sound on the exhalation. It doesn't have to be very loud.

Sound works from within the body. It is spreading the vibration and helps the energy spread and rise to the level of the heart and throat, which is exactly what we need to activate the full-body orgasm.

Making sound is the fastest way to move the energy. Do not undervalue it.

As you make a sound you activate more of Shakti, in other words — Life in you.

6. Movement

Breath, sound and movement are the three anchors that we have full access to at all times, and all three of those are activating Life in us.

As you relax and soften your body, as you breathe deeper it is very natural for spontaneous movement to arise from inside. It simply feels delicious to move in a sensual way.

Here, the same as with sound, you might have some inhibitions or shame coming up. Give it a go. I promise, a moment will come when you won't be able to resist the spontaneous expression just because it feels so good.

Breath, sound and movement help us generate more energy in ourselves. They are also allowing this energy to move through us, thus spreading the sensation, the pleasure and opening us up to the incredible full-body orgasm.

7. Yoni/Lingam activation

Yoni is the Sanskrit word for vulva, and lingam - for penis.

Our genitals are the seat of our sexual energy. It is our place of power, both emissive (for a man) and receptive (for a woman).

Our genitals need to be activated. If we have not done any conscious work on activating them in most cases they are numb. Usually, we do not realize that that's the case because we have nothing to compare it with.

78

This numbness is the result of the disconnect that we historically have from our sexuality due to societal taboos, shame and conditioning.

How do we activate the genitals? By bringing awareness to them. By making our genitals a place where we rest. By exploring and massaging them.

As you activate your genitals, a lot more of your sexual power becomes available to you, and therefore, deeper orgasms become accessible.

8. Trust

Another essential key for a full-body orgasm is **trust**. In order to orgasm, you need to trust. You need to open to Life. You need to surrender. Even though it may sound very blunt and even scary, this is truth: to have big orgasms we need to go to those places that may look very scary to the mind. There is nothing scary about those places for your being though, for that is the Life that you are. Because orgasm is a manifestation of Life in its depth. And actually, fear is a good sign. It means we are getting out of our comfort zone. It means, we are onto something that stretches us. We are onto something good.

Trust is based on a deep inner knowing that you are taken care of by the Divine. It is as simple as that. Yet, it is rare to meet a person who really trusts.

Because as soon as something happens that takes us out of our comfort zone, most people judge it as negative. They blame the world or feel pity for themselves. It is not always easy to recognize that there is wisdom even in things that don't seem to be desirable. When we can see that, it means that we know what trust is.

To come to those deep life-changing orgasms we need to open. And open completely.

Often a fear will come, and you might hear yourself thinking: *"But what if I open so much, and then this person leaves me?"*

In fact, you are never opening to a person.
You are always opening to the Divine.

Even when it looks like you are opening to a person, you are opening to the Divine within that person.

Without opening nothing makes sense. Real tantric orgasms come only with opening. Real Life comes only with opening. Real love comes only with opening.

See how you can make yourself available to that opening. How can you drop your guard? We tend to have the protective shield that keeps us cut off from the depth of Life.

Every time we choose to open, we are making ourselves more accessible to love.

Yes, you might feel hurt and you may experience uncomfortable emotions. Actually, let me re-phrase this: you will at times feel hurt and betrayed. It is inevitable. It is the nature of the world

— the world is a place of changes. We may try to wait for that one person to whom we can give ourselves completely, whom we can trust. Until that happens, we are waiting, unblissful and closed. Unless we are choosing to trust, completely, right now, we will be always hurt by change.

I know of no greater happiness than opening myself to infinity, dying every moment in the openness of trust, in the openness of love.

You can surrender as if you were dying right now. What is left after you've surrendered everything?

Feel as deeply as you possibly can. Live open to that feeling, alive as Life itself, no matter how horrible or beautiful the world seems. There is absolutely no reason to wait for a better time to open because life is happening right now.

The fear pales in comparison to what happens to your being each time you choose to open. The more you open, the more you love. This shift in mindset is a prerequisite for those deep orgasms.

You see, we cannot separate those things, it all comes together.

We cannot be completely shut off in life and then orgasm in bed like crazy.

That's why men and women who are fully orgasmic always stand out in the crowd. It is seen in their eyes, in their presence, in the way they walk and speak. You have everything you need to be one of those people. It is your birthright.

More thoughts on the Etheric Body

As I mentioned above, we can use sex to awaken our body of energy, to get activated, to start living fully.

As we are developing our etheric body, we notice that it works like a muscle. Through its development it becomes an organ of pleasure. You may arrive at a state where you feel that your pleasure becomes greater and greater. It builds over minutes and hours and you can enter into an orgasmic state that lasts for days!

Between those orgasms you will feel your etheric body is heightened and vibrant as well as solid, contained and stable.

When we go through the process of re-framing sex and orgasm at first we might feel like nothing is happening. It will feel rather faint in the beginning. However, it is a matter of gradual cultivation. In time, it will become so big, other forms of pleasure will become pale in comparison.

As you train yourself to experience tantric orgasms, you will start experiencing waves of pleasure. The guideline is to not make a distinction between etheric orgasm and the wave of etheric pleasure. When the waves start, call it etheric orgasm.

If you are more open to pleasure, it is your job to educate your partner about what is going on. It is possible to touch a wrong part and stop the orgasm from building!

The more you open to etheric orgasm, the less there tend to

be things that block your pleasure. Things that block your pleasure are usually nothing but conditioning related to past trauma.

The more we cultivate our etheric body, the more it becomes fluid. Energy is meant to move. As you are constantly letting your energetic body move and exercise, it becomes strong. It fights any virus or bacteria and it is the key to an excellent immune system. Also, a strong etheric body will affect your astral and mental bodies, making your whole being, your system more fluid with far less tendency to get stuck and hold onto the past.

The gift of feeling it all

How I invite you to go into sex, is very much how I invite you to go into Life. With a full "yes" to it all.

What does it mean?

Here is an example:

At times during sex we might hit against heaviness and boredom. I experienced this — I went through a a phase of getting really bored in sex. My way out was the way through. I was dropping deeper into the heaviness, even into the boredom. Instead of trying to push it away or changing it, I was dropping deeper into whatever sensations were there, even if it was boredom.

It lasted for months! It also coincided with being in a long-term relationship. There were other things that had to move in that relationship. Sex was reflecting those things, as it always does in relationships. I would get aroused, but then I would get bored. I was also pressing myself to experience it fully. I dropped deeper than the story of my mind of how sex should be. I had to drop even the story that sex should be exciting. I had to make a choice to move from the need to have a strong physical sensation, which I used to associate with the only way to orgasm, just as many people do.

Even though I was always a highly sexual person, thanks to that period of "sexual boredom" I saw that I was not accessing even half of what was possible. I started accessing my etheric body. I started teaching myself to feel the emotions in the body. Yes, we can feel the energy of our emotions in the body.

We have access to our mind. We are, to one degree or another, familiar with our emotions. We train our physical bodies. But, our etheric body is the weak link. When, in fact, it is through a strong etheric body that we can experience spirit within ourselves, not away from us. We can experience Tantra. We can experience God in this creation.

We have the challenge to awaken our etheric body because it is asleep. We can teach our etheric body to be intelligent. We can train it so highly that we can perceive spaces, people and objects; we can help our digestion; we can move our sexual energy — all through the intelligence of the etheric body.

In the beginning, it takes will to remind ourselves to stay present to the feelings. We need to know that it is, in fact, very simple. Activated energetic body is the key to an expanded

84

Life. When you make love, avoid grasping for pleasure —
make a commitment to stay in the erotic field even if it feels
like nothing is happening. There is no problem with strong
physical movement, you need only to remember not to grasp.
First and foremost — you need to be completely present. This
is the only way to access your expansion.

At the same time, presence is also being cultivated through
these practices. Develop a sense of wonder for sexual energy.
Where is it going to take you this time? What can you access
through this opening?

It is mesmerizing, really.

Kundalini: Awakening the snake

The coiled snake is sitting at the level of your root charka. In
Tantra, this snake is called kundalini, which is nothing but our
raw sexual energy.

Often she awakens even without us knowing.

Awakening kundalini is considered to be a mystical experience.
It is mystical because it shifts our consciousness, it shifts our
life, it awakens us from sleep.

Our society and the majority of people in the world that we
live in are sleeping. We see corrupt leaders; abuse of power;
complete disconnection from nature and from each other;
games of comparison and competition; manipulation — all
these are products of being asleep to the totality of our being
and our true nature. Sleep means that we forgot who we are,

85

we forgot our true nature and that our nature is love.

We don't see things for what they really are because we have become numb.

Awakening our energy and awakening as human beings come hand in hand. These are not little things.

Through the things that you learn in this book, it may look like we are just doing some practices, that we are learning how to have more pleasure in life, how to become orgasmic. In reality, it goes far beyond that.

That's why I am so passionate about this work — it is actually bringing us to an awakening on the largest scale. This work takes us beyond our conditioning that the sleeping mind has created and that we grew up believing in. We are using eroticism, sexuality and pleasure as a portal to align with the Divine.

What happens as kundalini awakens?

For some people it's a very scary experience.

What happens is that Shakti, the primordial life awakens within. This experience will be particularly intense for people who have been deeply asleep in a large part of their consciousness, those who have been drowning in unconscious patterns. In this case, it can be very scary, and it can really shake your life and turn everything you have ever known upside down. Often this happens as a result of an intensive practice.

All of a sudden, all the power that you didn't know existed within you awakens. This can feel very scary. But it is only scary because your power becomes accessible. You are accessing your Life, finally. Finally, you are becoming available to the magnitude of your being.

It might also be a mild experience. It may manifest as goose bumps on your skin or waves of heat. It can also be highly orgasmic.

In fact, it is always orgasmic. It takes a willingness, though, to recognize it as such.

Whenever I have an orgasm, I have a kundalini awakening experience. It happens a lot, and often — outside of sexual interaction.

We can experience kundalini awakening when we are being exposed to incredible beauty, for example, watching a sunset or listening to magnificent music that touches the strings of our soul.

Yes, a sunset can be orgasmic!

Kundalini can awaken when we are being touched by something, enjoying something or experiencing strong emotions.

There are techniques in yoga that are designed specifically to awakening our kundalini. I spent many years intensively practicing hatha and kundalini yoga.

When I was having my first kundalini awakening experiences, it was a very bumpy ride. It literally felt that I was being stretched beyond my capacity. It was making me extremely emotional. My suppressed anger was surfacing and making me extremely uncomfortable! That's the nature of an awakened life — you have to be present to everything and you have nowhere to hide. Physically, it felt uncomfortable too — I was experiencing burning and itching all over my body.

I was living in practice mode for five years. My practice was my job. I was firmly committed to my yogic life and that was it. I was doing purification practices daily, the more intense ones - every two weeks.

I do not recommend doing intensive practice if you are living a normal life and not eating a very clean diet. It may even be dangerous. I know someone who ended up having a psychotic episode because of this.

Please do not pursue intensive practices if you are not prepared.

However, if you take consideration of your lifestyle, if you know that you are emotionally stable and grounded then in one way or another, work with your energy. Big recommendation is to stay away from recreational drugs and alcohol, as well as from smoking, because this interferes with your capacity for energetic awakening. If you are physically active, and are conscious in your dietary choices, I would recommend mild practices that work gently on kundalini awakening.

The full-body energetic tantric orgasm: exercise.

You will be combining breath and movement to awaken the central channel of your being, called shushumna nadi. It is positioned along your spine, starting at the perineum and ends on top of your head.

Visualize this channel and the movement of energy along it.

Remember this: where the mind goes — energy flows. For most people at first it is about using the mind. We have a great asset as human beings, it is called attention: we can manipulate it, use it, connect with it. As your energetic body awakens more and more it becomes intelligent. You will be moving the energy itself.

Bring your awareness to the perineum. Feel into the energy of this area, feel the denseness of the energy in that area, then move your attention to your pelvis. Scan your pelvis, what can you feel? Can you feel coolness, warmth or heat in your pelvis? Do you perceive any colours?

Next, bring your attention up — feel or imagine that light is rising up your spine, all the way to the top of your head.

As you inhale, squeeze the muscles of your pelvic floor known as the the PC muscles and direct your energy upwards.
As you exhale, relax your whole body and feel or imagine how the energy spreads throughout your whole body.

Then add movement. Move your pelvis forwards as you move your energy up. Move your pelvis backwards as you let the energy spread.

Practice this whenever you like throughout the day. And definitely bring it into your love making and self-pleasure practice.

The Silent Orgasm

Orgasm can look like a volcanic explosion. It can come together with intense shaking of the body, tears, laughter, roaring, howling, intense high pitch or deep sounds... It can look like anything, really.

Orgasm can also look like nothing. It may feel like deep waves are moving through you, but you are motionless, completely silent, still. You may even stop breathing. However, you are experiencing enormous connection, enormous expansion, enormous freedom, absolute bliss. It may happen during intercourse or outside of sexual experience. I call it the Silent Orgasm.

The wild and primal expression is usually very healing as it helps move energy that may have been stuck.

Although during the silent orgasm the intensity experienced has even greater voltage, however you are capable of riding it, like the great warrior - goddess Durga who is usually depicted riding a tiger. You are riding the intensity and opening into the vastness of your consciousness through it, yet you remain completely internalized and silent.

11
From Physical, Grasping Sex to Expansion into the State of Beingness.

Generally, people think that there are only a couple of ways of creating pleasure.

Nothing can be further from truth.

The potential within conscious sex is glorious. Conscious sex can be our means to opening to the Divine. Tantric sex can expand us like nothing else.

There is a belief that many people share that good sex equals hard sex. Some people even believe that a woman needs to be taken really hard so that she is sexually fulfilled and stops being bitchy and "naggy". In fact, there is a time for such rawness and pounding as the expression of our primal side. However it is only a little fraction of what is possible in sex, of how deep we can go in sex — and oh, we can go really deep!

This view is due to three reasons:

1.   Porn

For most people it is the only source of sexual education available. Porn is focused on producing intense stimulation of the brain and therefore, a quick release.

2.   Instinctual desire to procreate

Nature has an agenda: it wants us to procreate. Life wants more of Life, which may not always be our choice.

According to nature's programming the male will want to release the semen (and its best if it happens as fast as possible so that more females can be impregnated). The female will be drawing the semen out of the male (and she is equipped with an energetic know-how and has all sorts of tricks for that – see chapter on Woman's role in Male Orgasm). Yet, since ancient times, we know that sex is there not only for us to procreate. It is also there for our pleasure, through which we can grow, tap into truly sacred realms of our being, expand into our Eros and turn into a better version of ourselves.

3.   Shame

Having been in the tantric and conscious sexuality field for many years, I can testify that there are many, MANY layers of sexual shame.

Shame is usually completely unconscious. It becomes a program that controls us. So what does hard sex have to do with shame? Shame makes us want to throw off sexual energy, and as soon as possible. When hard pounding is involved we are likely to finish fast, and therefore get rid of this big, intense energy.

Are there ways to expand through sex rather than feed the programming we have been given?

Yes.

Instead of going for the grasping type of sex, aimed at producing intense physical sensation, slow it down. Give your sensations space. Stay present. Don't follow your mind. Stay present. Allow feelings to build. Allow your heart to open into the space that is being cultivated even without you doing anything.

A powerful technique that I love:

> *Connect your genitals ("plug in") and stay still. Hold each other, maintain eye contact, synchronize your breath, and stay still. Feel into your genitals, breathe deeply all the way to the genitals as sex becomes a meditation.*

> *Stay very present with the sensations in your genitals. Let them do their job, trust me: they know what to do.*

> *The main thing to remember: drop all expectations. Even if the penis becomes soft — it's totally fine. Stay with what arises. Become mesmerized.*

A note on soft penis in lovemaking

We tend to think that lovemaking requires a hard penis. As soon as the man is no longer erect most couples end the lovemaking. Of course, if he ejaculated he will have the resting period as there is a loss of energy. But if he didn't ejaculate and the cock is soft - is it a sign to stop? My invitation is to reframe this idea that to make love a man needs to be hard. My invitation is to learn to trust the intelligence of the body. When the cock becomes soft don't label it as a failure or an ending. Stay with it and find new ways of making love. Find the edge that this softness is inviting you to. Feel its vulnerability. It is a soft heart that allows a soft cock. But can you handle the intensity of the soft heart?

A soft penis feels delicious inside of a yoni that is awake. I encourage you to practice soft penetration from time to time, and simply rest in this connection. Spontaneously, it may happen that the penis starts uncoiling inside of the yoni. And it feels wonderful.

I once had a lover who had a very large penis. He was so virile it seemed like he could get hard anywhere, anytime. And his erections could last for hours. Now, this sounds like any man's dream. But I have to tell you that I was excited about this in the beginning, but it didn't take long before I stopped enjoying it. I started longing for more softness and tenderness. I was actually longing to feel the softness of his penis. I realized I couldn't access the vulnerability of this man, because he was not in touch with it himself.

The longer we stayed together the more he dropped deeper and deeper into his heart. At some point through our connection and practice he softened beyond what he had ever experienced. This was when his erections stopped being so intense. He didn't become less powerful as a lover, he actually became more powerful, because he started allowing his heart to be connected to his sex. This coincided with his increased capacity for powerful full body orgasms.

12
Orgasmic Healing

Orgasmic energy is healing in its essence

One of the reasons for the cultivation of our capacity for deep energetic orgasms is that it produces healing. When your full body is orgasming, when you are not tensing up, not restricting the energy, not pushing it out, but taking all in, letting it wash through you you are also healing yourself.

In fact, a full sexual experience is the most fundamental way of healing ourselves. It releases all the tensions and stress that is built up in us.

Many people, both men and women, have experienced sexual abuse, which may have left deep scars. I have witnessed the incredible healing that happens to those people when they open up to the power of sexual energy.

With sexual healing, we solve problems at the level where they were created — at the very root.

Referring back to the model of the Five Bodies of a Human Being, the tantric orgasm is happening at the level of all bodies. In the very end of this book I will reveal to you how even the fifth, causal body is being activated in orgasm.

Now let's focus on the healing aspect.

It's been proven that before we manifest any physical symptoms, the disease actually exists in the energetic body. Something in our energetic field gets compromised and only after that does the physical body gets affected.

In Kirlian photography it is possible to see the disease even before in manifests. It is possible to see that the energy field of the liver is disturbed, and only after that the person will discover that they have liver disease.

Therefore, when we are actively working on strengthening our energetic body we are offering a tremendous gift to our physical body too.

We can train our energetic body with orgasm. The more you train the deeper your orgasms become.

In my own life, I have observed that every time I orgasm I go to deeper and deeper places. So there really is no end to the orgasmic opening. The end is when we are actually orgasming into liberation.

When we are orgasming, we are nourishing, replenishing and empowering our energetic field. It is like taking a shower of light, washing our system and releasing any gunk. Through it we are also restoring anything that is not intact.

Just by allowing the orgasm to happen, the energy will be naturally going where it needs to go.

For example, I love the powerful practice of microcosmic orbit breathing.

We breath along the central channel of our body, and the energy gets distributed to places where it is needed, therefore providing healing.

Basic Elements of Sex Magic

The second way of healing through orgasm is when we are directing the energy to where we need it. We direct the energy to the place where we already have a problem.

Let's say you have pain in your shoulder. Then, during the time when you feel the orgasmic energy running through the body and the waves of pleasure start to take over, you send some extra energy to your shoulder. You can also guide the energy with your hands, just marking the movement of the energy. This is a very powerful way to heal.

13
Amrita — The Nectar of the Goddess

Let me warn you: it's going to get wet and juicy. Yet, there is nothing to fear. On the contrary, female ejaculation is an incredibly empowering phenomenon for a woman. If you have never experienced it, I have great news — you can learn. In fact, anyone can learn to squirt.

What is female ejaculation?

Sometimes it is referred to as squirting or gushing. In Tantra, it is referred to as kalas, which indicates the esoteric nature of this phenomenon and its connection with the cycles of the Moon. My favorite description is the beautiful word *amrita*, which means *Divine nectar*.

In ancient scriptures it is said that when *amrita* flows, the earth and all its inhabitants are healed. Are you getting the feel of it? Mmm.

What happens on the physiological level? Female ejaculation is a physiological action usually associated with orgasm and is completely different from urination. It is associated with the release of what in a man is called prostatic enzymes, such as PSA (prostate-specific antigen).

Ancient Taoist texts talk about three different types of *amrita*, which come from the urethra, the walls of the vagina and the womb through the cervix.

It may come out from the same hole as urine does, that's why some people assume it's pee. It may also come out of the Bartholin's glands and the Skene's glands, which are located at the level of the G-spot. And, it may ooze out of the vaginal walls. In any case — it's not pee.

There are also scientific studies that have proven that liquid that gets secreted during female ejaculation experience is not urine. There might be a little bit of urine in case of ejaculation that is occurring through the pee hole. What proves that it is not pee is the smell. Female ejaculation smells wonderfully — and it also tastes really good.

The amount of liquid varies from woman to woman and from day to day. I know from my own experience that sometimes I will trickle a few drops, and other times, the amount can be quite significant. Sometimes, women can even soak the entire bed! These large amounts are truly amazing. Doctors can't give an explanation to why it happens. Medical understanding accepts that some liquid can come out from the Skene's gland, that's how female ejaculation is understood. But the abundant fluid released cannot be explained by conventional medicine.

Here is a hint. Female ejaculation is a mystical experience. It is directly related to your connection with the cycles of the Moon. If you pay attention, you will notice that on some days of the month squirting is easier than on others.

Tantra says that ability to produce *kalas* is a woman's step into paranormal powers. It is the physical manifestation of sexual energy. How cool is that? The great news is that any woman can do it.

The liquid that is secreted is very precious. It has lots of healing properties, the results of which I've witnessed many times. Tantric people try not to waste a drop of it. They will drink it or rub it on the skin. It feels and tastes beautiful.

Ok, Sofia, you sold it. How do I get there?

First of all, you need to be very relaxed and very aroused. Do everything you can to empty your mind. A great skill that we learn with the *yoni egg practice* is the pushing out with the vaginal muscles. (Yoni egg practice is an ancient Taoist practice that works on strengthening the vaginal muscles). This skill is handy when it comes to female ejaculation. It's great to train these muscles.

Since it is such a mysterious manifestation of our sexuality, it's quite mysterious how *amrita* can be triggered. Generally, there are three ways women can experience it:

1. For those women who are only starting to work on sensitizing their yoni, most commonly the *amrita* will result from prolonged and firm stimulation of the urethral sponge, around the area of A-spot and G-spot. In this case, normally

101

some or all of the *amrita* is secreted from the urethra, and some — from the walls of the vagina, around the G-spot. (The G-spot is located about four - six centimeters inside the vagina on the frontal wall. The A-spot is located a little higher, just in front of the cervix, also on the frontal wall. The frontal wall is on the side of your pubic bone, the back wall is on the side of your anus.)

The stimulation has to be rhythmical and thrusting. If you are taking yourself there — it's great to use toys designed for G-spot stimulation. Or, if you have a wonderful partner or a friend who is happy to assist you in this blissful experience — fingers do a better job than a cock.

Don't put pressure on yourself or your partner— have fun with it. Keep practicing and one day the fountain of immortality will show its essence to you through your own yoni.

2. Sometimes you may experience such state of openness that *amrita* just gushes spontaneously. It may even happen outside of intercourse. It's pretty awesome, I must say. Usually, this type of *amrita* is coming directly from the womb, through the cervix.

3. Other times *amrita* will be secreted from all possible places: from the urethra, from the vaginal walls, from the A- and G-spots and from the womb all at once or in cycles. The nature of the feminine is wild, and so is our sexual energy.

For me it is easiest to experience *amrita* at will when I am highly aroused and I feel that my yoni is energetically full. I squat, stand up or sit on my knees. It's more difficult if I lie on my back. Then I would squeeze my entire yoni and have either my own or my partner's fingers moving back and forth (between the frontal and back wall of the vagina), or a penis gently tapping this area. This helps to build up the waters. Then after a few moments when I will feel that I want to release *amrita*, I will stop the movement and gently push out with my yoni.

What's stopping you?

Probably your mind. You might think to yourself: *"I cannot possibly do this. What will my partner think of me?"* Many women think this way, not knowing that they are pushing away an experience that is incomparable to anything else. I hope that once you have read about the nature of this precious liquid, you will change your opinion. And please do educate your partner about it.

You might also think: "Imagine all the mess that I will create. I may even spoil the bed." I know a couple who bought a rubber boat for this purpose. You don't need a rubber boat, but you can get creative: use a towel under your pelvis, puddle-proof pads or do it in the bathtub.

You might have more fears and thoughts but the important thing to remember here is: these thoughts are your inner saboteur, it is your resistance — a part of you that wants to stay small and doesn't want to experience deep pleasure because it knows — you won't be the same person after that.

Do everything you can to make it comfortable for your mind but then if things are not going the way you planned, let it go, don't react to the provocations of your mind.

When you are pushing out physically, you actually don't have to push out energetically at the same time. You can be pushing out with your yoni and yet circulating the energy along the microcosmic orbit for example. Microcosmic orbit is a circular path that begins at the level of your perineum then travels up your back and over your head and back to your pelvis.

Another thing to know is that *amrita* doesn't have to always come together with physical pushing. Sometimes it may come without any effort whatsoever, just a super high level of arousal and openness of the yoni. Ahh, just writing about this feels so juicy!

Here is how it feels from a man's perspective:

"I lay in shavasana after being bathed in the holy waters of a white snowflake melting onto me. In the flow and fire I was hypnotized by her eyes rolled back, escaping into ecstasy, unable to look into mine. I lay with a loss for words and unable to move having remained present for such precious depths of desire being poured onto my shaft and body. I lay there anchored deep into the earth's core while absorbing the sweet nectar of life through my pores. What beauty in this analogy. The core of the earth flowed as lava and conforms to this earthly body of an island. And I too, drenched by the flow coming from the core of her mystical being, am formed by amrita's unseen ravine. I have been baptized and sanctified in the pleasures of Life. Ode to the heavenly healing waters in the belly of my silence."

14
Anal Orgasm

Now, this is a big taboo. Anal penetration with either fingers, dildos or a cock is not something we speak about every day. (Well, sometimes I do, but it's not the reality for most people, right?)

We sure do have a lot of reservations even upon hearing the word "anus".

So, let's dive right in!

Ever heard of the term: "anal-retentive personality"?

Sometimes we think that we need to do this and that in order to be this way or that way. I'd say, what if **we start by relaxing the anus first?**

See what happens after that!

If you were to bring your awareness to your anus now, you would most probably notice that it is tight and firmly clenched.

We can take baby steps to feeling more comfortable with our anus. The next time you are taking a shower, put some soap on your finger and gently insert it in your anus. The Taoist would also encourage us to do rotations — nine clockwise and nine counter-clockwise.

After that, wash your finger thoroughly. Do this every day. That's it. Not too big of a deal, right?

You'll be surprised at how deep the effects of this simple and (fairly) innocent practice go over time.

It is a great way for you to learn how much tension you are actually holding in your anus. This also does something great for your health. This is the best thing you can do to prevent hemorrhoids. Olive or coconut oil will work even better than soap.

This should be one of the tools in your erotic toolbox because anal play is also an incredibly juicy thing that can add lots of spice to your sex life.

Some women reach the most profound orgasms through anal stimulation, in some cases even deeper than those they can reach though vaginal penetration. For men it is usually an intense experience, that can build into profound orgasmic state.

It is not something that is openly accepted in our homophobic culture but you'd be surprised to know that the male G-spot is the prostate gland — accessible through the anus.

It is incredibly powerful for a man to experience what it is like to be penetrated. To let go to a degree that most men never have the chance to let go in Life, to surrender to a very deep pleasure and to let go into something that seems so edgy to the mind.

You learn how to open up in all areas of your Life. You learn how to relax and surrender and fall into the unknown.

Anal stimulation or sex is highly recommended for people who have a strong tendency for control and for people who tend to feel heavy and tired.

Normally, anal sex is an incredibly powerful experience because it takes a lot of vulnerability to do it. An anal orgasm is a very unique sensation and incredibly powerful! For women it may come together with clitoral orgasm.

To sum it up: Anal play is transformative and it will give you an experience of a larger degree of freedom as you get a taste of releasing control.

Hopefully, you've got the *why* by now.

Are you ready to move on to the *how*?

First of all, not having a partner is not an excuse just in the same way that being ecstatic and orgasmic does not require a partner. We need to learn to **own our pleasure.**

By all means go for it by yourself.

If you have a beloved or a dear friend with whom you would like to practice this — that's great too. It will take your intimacy to a whole new level.

First of all, use a lot of oil. You can choose a natural lubricant but I particularly love coconut oil for its texture, plus it has antibacterial and antifungal properties.

A full-body massage is great preparation. It's especially good to focus on massaging out any tension in the lower back, hips and bum. Really spend time on those areas, including a good ten minutes just on the bum. Give lots of attention to the sacrum —the triangular bone that you can feel just above the top of the bum crack. It's great to offer lots of conscious touch to the sacrum. It can be highly orgasmic too!

It is a great idea to not only massage the whole body of your beloved but to also focus on their genitals.

When you feel it is time to approach the anus, by all means, **go slow.** The anus consists of two circular groups of muscles that create two rings: the external sphincter and the internal sphincter. The outer sphincter is a voluntary muscle and the inner is an involuntary one. This means that you can totally control the first ring (the outer sphincter) as it is a matter of deep relaxation and surrender. The second ring (the inner sphincter) may take a little longer to relax and here you just have to be patient.

Before actual penetration, you need to make sure that your partner is deeply relaxed. It's best to move into anal stimulation after a good session of either yoni or lingam massage or even penetrative sex. The more pleasure they feel, the easier the process of de-armoring their anus will be. When your partner is ready, gently approach the anus. Make sure to use a lot of oil or lubricant. Very importantly — take time. Anal massage will liberate a lot of stuck energy and can even trigger anal orgasms, which cannot really be compared to anything else.

How to massage the anus?

I will say this again: go very slowly and with a lot of lubrication. Unlike the vagina, the anus does not produce any lubrication, so there is really no way to overdo it here.

- As you are sliding in with one finger (either the index or the middle finger) keep eye contact with your partner if possible and only proceed with penetration when you feel she/he is open to it.
- At times, it is good to pause and hold the space in stillness.
- Make tiny circles with your fingertip on the walls of the anus.
- Continuously encourage your partner to breathe deeply. This will help him/her to let go more deeply.
- With your deep presence, slide your finger up and down along the frontal wall of the anus. (The frontal side is the one that's closer to the belly button, the back is the one that's closer to the coccyx).
- With your deep presence, slide your finger up and down along the back wall of the anus.
- Communication is key. As recipient it is very

important that you actually share what you are experiencing. Feel free to ask for more of this or less of that. If you feel pain or pleasure —— communicate it. Ask your partner to pause if it gets too intense. Ask your partner to speed up if that's what you are feeling.

• Be even more careful when you are removing the finger — do it very, very slowly and only through relaxation.

• This is very important! Make sure never to touch the yoni of the woman with the same finger that you used for anal play — the bacteria may cause a urinary tract infection, and this is a very unpleasant thing to deal with.

The best position for anal stimulation

The best position for anal stimulation is the one that works for you. Generally, having the recipient lying on his/her back might be a good way to start because it is a less vulnerable position than being on all fours, for example, and therefore it can help them feel more relaxed.

In case you think I am going to avoid the elephant in the room, you don't know me well enough.

So, what about shit?
Yes, we generally use the anus to shit. (I literally can see you blushing now. You're cute.)

When you play with somebody's anus, you may encounter shit.

If your inner Queen Victoria cannot stand this thought, it means that anal play would be especially good for you.

Because this inner queen is nothing but an inner puritanical control freak. At the same time, the anus and the lower part of the rectum actually have very little fecal material in them, which means it tends to not be nearly as dirty as you think.

You may see some shit on your finger/dildo or lingam. What you do with it is go to the bathroom and wash it off. In case of anal sex, do use a condom. Once you are finished, you simply take off the condom and throw it away.

If you are playing using your fingers, you can use latex gloves if that saves the day for you.

You can also play it safe and have the recipient have an enema with water beforehand. Don't overdo it, it is not very healthy. But there is nothing wrong with doing it occasionally.

So find your level of comfort with each other. See how much you are willing to stretch it. Remember, there is never a reason to push yourself into something you don't want. Anal play is something that can open you up to incredible pleasure and expand you like nothing else, but you need to be willing to go there. Don't do it just to please your partner. If this is something you want to either receive or offer — do share it with your partner, their reaction might surprise you.

15
Self-Love Is Where it Starts.
Body Image.

I remember being embarrassed by my belly, thinking that
it should be small. I was doing lots of exercise to hide it,
to make it flat.

I want to reach out to that younger me, take her in my lap and
kiss all her confusion out of her head.

We get so brainwashed about the way we should look. The
media is selling us this image of a polished look, where there is
nothing extra, nothing soft and therefore nothing human. We
are being sold this sterile, unsexual and rigid image.

Well, you might argue with the sexual part because sex sells.
Even when selling nappies for newborns, you sometimes see
a picture of a blonde in high heels. But even this "sexual" is a
very diminished and sterile kind of sexual.

Our eroticism is free in its nature. It cannot fit into those
concepts. Our eroticism is real, it cannot be sterile! Look at

112

nature, nature is so erotic! Are you going to tell a tree that its trunk needs to be a bit slimmer?

I love my belly. And ever since I started loving my belly, I have been receiving compliments from others about it and even quite frequently. The belly is our emotional center. I also know that my belly feels so nice because my emotions are not stagnant but they flow freely. I take space in this world and therefore, I am not trying to hide my belly. When we don't repress our bodies, and don't repress our emotions, when we give space to our bellies, to our emotions, to our physicality, our eroticism — they become beautiful energetically and therefore, physically too.

When I was a teenager I had a pretty poor body image. I didn't find myself beautiful at all. I was constantly comparing myself to other girls. I always thought that they were more beautiful — or more ugly — than I was. It was as if there was a certain standard of beauty into which everyone should fit. One day I remember looking in the mirror and I thought to myself: *"What if this, what I see now, is beauty?"* I don't know where I downloaded that from back then, but I must say, it was pretty on point.

So let us all learn from 16-year-old me. Go look in the mirror now and after a few minutes ask yourself: *"What if this* **is** *beauty?"*

You might be interested to know that over 90% of people do not like their bodies. That's a lot of people.

If we are too focused on our body image and insecurities, we can't be really present with our lover. We are in our mind.

113

There's no way to surrender when we are caught in our mind. If we can't surrender, we can't fully experience intimacy nor can we truly orgasm. If we do not feel safe in our body, we cannot fully open ourselves to feel sexual pleasure.

Have you noticed that some people who have great physical attributes do not strike us as particularly attractive and others who are not that physically beautiful come across as absolutely gorgeous? I've observed dozens of examples of this. I believe that the key here is self-love.

Loving ourselves expands our beauty.

Loving ourselves means accepting ourselves in the totality of our being and loving all of the features we have — the perfect, the average and the ugly. We are all humans, so we each have parts of ourselves that we don't approve of. We must embrace these parts especially to be truly gorgeous. We have to embrace our strengths and weaknesses to be truly beautiful and attractive.

A great way to start feeling beautiful is to observe people who you find attractive, and question, what is so different about them compared to others? It may be the way they laugh, the way the hold themselves as they walk, the way they sit or move their hands as they speak. Then see how you can incorporate this in your own life, it's not that difficult after all. Many of us learn really well through transmission. If the situation allows — have the courage to approach that person and ask them for some tips. What is it they do that radiance is just oozing out?

Most importantly — we all need to learn to enjoy ourselves. When people are enjoying themselves, they are beautiful. Pleasure in life, satisfaction and frequent orgasms add to our glow.

Often, other people's criticizing comments about our looks can leave deep scars. This is especially true if it happened in our childhood. Everything a child experiences sinks right into the subconscious. Some seemingly small incidents may result in huge body issues. That means that you don't have a poor body image because of the way you look but the way people made you feel about your body or yourself. It is important to acknowledge that, and choose not to be affected by it anymore. Nothing can determine your destiny and the way you feel about yourself unless you allow it.

Every person can have their own kind of beauty, if they are willing to look for it. If we don't enjoy our own spirit, sensuality and personality, we can never be as beautiful as we could be. It's really hard to be beautiful when we're trying to fit in to some societal norms. We should make our own rules and cultivate our own beauty.

Here are a few practices that will help you develop self-love.

First tip: Open to your wounds. Ask yourself: *"When was the first time I felt bad about myself/my body? Why did I feel bad? Who made me feel bad?"* This is not about blaming anyone but to see clearly when and why you were wounded. Only then it is possible to heal. It might bring up some early painful memories, perhaps from your childhood. Write them down. Write down the way you felt at the time and the way it makes you feel now and the way you feel it's limiting you now. Often a process like this can help a lot. Then you need to decide that you want to change. And change.

Second tip: Treat your body as a precious thing. If you want others to love your body, you should love your body. Pamper it, scrub it with natural salts and massage it with essential oils. Your body will be grateful.

Third tip: Spend time naked, preferably surrounded by other naked people. Nude beaches, saunas and hot springs are all great places. This is incredibly healing and helps you to remember what human bodies actually look like. It is very rare that they look like the bodies we see on magazine covers.

Fourth tip: Look at your closet with a critical eye and throw away anything that makes you feel less than beautiful and also anything that you have not worn for over a year. This might change your life. Clothes actually carry energy. When we are holding onto our old clothes, we are also holding onto identities that may not reflect anything close to where we want to be in terms of our inner state.

Fifth tip: Ask yourself: *"How would my life be different if I were beautiful?"* Sometimes we don't do certain things in life because we think we are not good enough or not beautiful enough for them. So ask yourself this question and take some time to reflect on it and journal about it. Start doing the things you want to do now.

What would your closet look like if you were beautiful? Would you wear the same clothes? Would you eat the same food? Would you treat yourself the same way?

Sixth tip: Write yourself a love letter. Write down what you would love to receive from someone who adores you. Write down everything you love about yourself. Re-read it as often as you like, especially when you are feeling a little low.

Seventh tip: The mirror exercise. Stand naked in front of a big mirror and look at yourself. Look at yourself not with the eyes of a critic, but with the eyes of a lover. Love your body with your eyes. Look at yourself and breathe. Get used to it and remember: this is what beauty looks like.

Love for Self

Here is a very important part to the topic of self-love.

We can start loving ourselves beginning from our body, or we can start loving ourselves beginning from our Higher Self.

In the end, it doesn't matter.

But when we truly see and love our innate Divinity, we see everything within us as Divine, as worthy, as complete. From this big and expanded view, nothing within us ever needs to be fixed.

Love for Sex

Our genitals are de-sensitized.

To feel anything, we need to fuck and be fucked really hard.

Work on sensitizing our genitals is a big part of our conscious sexual work and one of the first things we all really need to look at.

For women, it's about resurrecting the yoni. When the yoni is sensitized, she opens up to the potential for pleasure that any yoni has.

Many women have de-sensitized themselves through the use of vibrators. Vibrators are de-sensitizing the vagina. Women using them may get used to the powerful vibration and overstimulation, which will decrease the level of her perception. We also de-sensitize ourselves by simply not paying attention to the vagina, not touching her, not getting to know her, not discovering any tense areas.

Men also need to work on sensitizing their genitals. Even though it might sound counter-intuitive because you may think that when a man is very sensitized he won't be able to last longer.

Even though you will last longer if you are de-sensitized or are thinking about football during love making, it won't give you as deep of an experience as you can have.

The solution is to work on building your awareness of sensation.

Men need to work on owning their genitals — owning their penis and testicles.

Performing daily stretches for the penis and balls. This means massaging the whole package. Adopt a habit of breathing into your pelvis and rest your consciousness in your penis.

It makes a huge difference in the way you show up if you show up in full ownership of your cock.

The amazing thing about this is that alongside with this work on your genitals, you are also working on releasing shame.

Once the genitals are sensitized, we realize that they don't need much stimulation at all.

We even discover that the less there is physical stimulation, the bigger the energetic charge.

The body is an amazing tool that we have. It is a true gateway. The more we are connected to our body, the deeper we are *embodied*, the more radiance is released through our Being alone.

It is so enjoyable to be in company of a person who is embodied. There is a sense of relaxation in their field that just makes you want to be around them.

Let's look a little deeper into the nature of our genitals, and the potential fully activated and sensitized genitals hold.

16
Yoni as the Source of Life

What does the word yoni mean? Yoni is translated from Sanskrit as the sacred temple. It refers to the female genitalia also known as the vulva. Some like to call her "pussy", but she has also been called many different names: "down there", "peepee", "hole", "cock pocket," "hairy mussel," "goodies," "honey pot," "kitty" and so on. I bet you will agree that none of it really expresses the magic, power and sacredness that is within the most feminine part of the female body.

What is the yoni, really? The yoni is a portal to Life. It is a place from where all Life originated. It is a cosmic gate through which we all came here. It is the most feminine part of a woman's body. It is the most receptive and the most sensitive part of a woman's body. So if we want to establish a deep connection with the feminine, the yoni is the place where we should start. It is such a mystical, mysterious, powerful and beautiful place.

In Taoist love poetry such terms as "golden lotus", "gates of paradise", "precious pearl", "'treasure" are used to describe the yoni.

The yoni is the **fount of immortality,** the inexhaustible Source of Life. We view the yoni as the original **location of Shakti, the potent kundalini energy.** When you excite her, she will be pleased and grant you every ecstasy. By giving the best, you receive the most.

The yoni is the **doorway** through which all humans must pass. The yoni is considered the entrance to both past and future.

When we hear people speak about feminine empowerment, there are so many concepts surrounding it, but not many people speak about the relationship of a woman to her vulva, her vagina, her yoni.

I strongly believe that that's where feminine empowerment should start.

So many women are completely disconnected from their yoni.

Many yonis hardly ever receive any loving touch. Even fewer receive praise or are looked at with awe and admiration.

Most yonis are not appreciated for the magical and mystical place they really are.

Without that, our yonis fall asleep. Or, sometimes they even fall into a coma.

It is crucial for all women to develop a profound and deep

relationship with their yoni. This is how we can own our power. This is how we can access our deepest wisdom and intuition.

Once there is this deep connection with the yoni, we start listening to her. Believe me, there are things she has to say.

Many women have no perception of their genitals or their vagina. They are simply not aware of this part of their body and therefore, they don't know about their orgasmic potential.

When I speak about prolonged lovemaking — one, two, three hours — many women feel cautious: "Hours of sex?! Even ten minutes is not really pleasant for me!" They associate sex with rubbing. There is nothing pleasant about it really.

Most women have either unpleasant sensations of burning or pain in the yoni or, they have a lack of perception of their yoni.

The biggest issue for women in the beginning (which is not such a big issue at all) is to develop their awareness, their pleasure and the sensitivity of their yoni. Women who are not trained, who did not dare to look at this area of their body — don't tend to experience nearly as much pleasure as is available to all of us.

We need to remember that opening to pleasure is not just about pleasure. Through our openness, we are cultivating mystical states. Our complete unconditional openness has the potential to bring us beyond anything we ever knew. If orgasm just comes and goes, it is not possible to enter these meditative and altered states.

Orgasm is not just about the clitoris and vagina. We need to learn to use our body as a temple where we can create states of consciousness.

Most women need to work on sensitizing the yoni, on recovering from their vaginal coma. Many women can't feel what's going on inside of them.

What do you do if you feel pain in the yoni during lovemaking? Most women will end lovemaking.

Is there another way?

Sore areas in vagina always correspond with frustration and other stuck emotions. These emotions usually manifest as painful spots in the vagina. Most women's yonis need to undergo some healing.

> *I have never been sexually abused and I never thought I needed any sexual healing. But now, after years of work on my sexuality, I can say that everybody needs sexual healing.*

Vaginal walls are very flexible and elastic. Think of childbirth — something the size of the head of a baby can pass through. The pain that the woman experiences during labor has to do with contractions of the uterus and the movement of bones but not with the vagina.

More than anything else, if a woman has pain it is a matter of relaxation and of releasing blockages of energy in the yoni.

123

Even tantric women tend to build tension in vagina because of stress or any unprocessed emotions. There is supposed to be no pain in the vagina. If there is pain, it means we need to work on it.

If your partner is very receptive, you can actually keep making love even if there is pain. Just go very slowly and be patient with your yoni. Allow her to open.

You can also visualize that his lingam transmits a healing light that enters your yoni, wraps her and penetrates and heals any sore areas.

Yoni Healing

There are a few amazing tools and practices we can do to begin this process of awakening and healing of our yoni, for example, **yoni massage, yoni dearmouring** and the **yoni egg practice.**

Yoni Massage

Yoni massage can be done with fingers or a dildo. A woman can do it by herself and it is also a great idea to receive it from a healer, a partner or a friend.

Before you approach the yoni make sure that you are warmed up and aroused. If that's not the case, the yoni simply won't open. Approaching a yoni that is closed may actually cause re-traumatising. During the massage itself, the woman will be noticing areas that are very pleasurable, and some that are numb. Some will carry discomfort or a burning sensation. It is

124

great to massage the painful spots. You will notice that you can actually massage the tension out. You may notice spots that feel like grains of rice or like little knots. By massaging them, you are dispersing the tension and opening them up.

Yoni Egg

The stone egg practice to strengthen the vagina emerged in ancient China. For a long time it was a secret practice, only available for the members of the royal family. Since ancient times, these practices have been used for improving the physical and spiritual health of a woman.

These eggs are often called yoni eggs.

The yoni egg practice is an incredibly sacred and deeply healing practice for women. It is also wonderful for training of the vaginal muscles.

The egg is an amazing tool that helps tone the lower abdomen and strengthen the muscles of the pelvic and urogenital diaphragms, which serve as a floor for all our vital organs. When these muscles are strong, they prevent leakage of our vital force and sexual energy and help us keep it under control.

Here are some of the benefits of the yoni egg practice:
- Increasing perception of your yoni and control over the vaginal muscles;
- Awakening your creative energy, passion and libido;
- Becoming A LOT more orgasmic;
- Gaining control of the perineum and all groups of the pelvic floor muscles;
- Giving a lot of pleasure to your man and helping

125

him with ejaculation control;
• Harmonizing your emotions and healing your relationship to intimacy and sexuality;
• Reducing PMS, menstrual cramps and breast discomfort;
• Reducing menopausal symptoms by increasing vaginal lubrication and balancing estrogen levels;
• Overcoming traumatic experiences of sexual abuse.

There are also vaginal exercises called Kegels, named after the person who developed them — Dr. Kegel. Initially, these exercises were developed for women who have difficulty controlling urination.

There are three main exercises:

1. Squeeze the yoni 50 times in a row as quickly as possible.
2. Squeeze the yoni for five seconds, hold it and relax for five seconds. Repeat a few times.
3. Push out with the muscles of the yoni, then relax. Repeat a few times.

It's great to teach yourself to isolate the muscles of the yoni from the thighs, butt and anus.

WARNING: It is very important not to overdo these exercises. It may actually be counterproductive and may make the yoni too tense and cause de-sensitization!

We don't want to create a yoni that is tight like a fist, we want the yoni to be alive, responsive and flexible.

Another great exercise that you can do right now is called Five Sacred Orifices. In this exercise you are learning to separate various areas of the yoni:
- the clitoris
- the urethra
- the vaginal opening
- the perineum
- the anus

Squeeze and relax each of these separately.

Yoni Worship

Yoni Puja

A yoni puja is a sacred tantric ritual during which the yoni is worshipped. We express adoration for the feminine principle. We express our complete love and appreciation of the feminine essence in all her forms.

This ritual originated in India, thousands of years ago. There are many various forms in which this ritual can be performed.

Important prerequisite for worshipping the yoni is the purification of the mind from worldly ideas about yoni, specifically, of the shame and guilt most of us carry.

With the yoni puja we express the reverence in front of the mystery of the Universe, of Shakti, the Divine mother. By worshipping the yoni we worship Shakti — the feminine essence, the innermost being of all women.

The ritual can be performed with a symbol, a sculpture or an object representing a yoni, or on a yoni in her living form.

A yoni puja can be an incredible gift that you can offer to your female partner or friend. A woman can also perform a yoni puja for herself.

It is extremely powerful to perform it on a real yoni. But, if you are not comfortable with it, or the circumstances are not appropriate for whatever reason, performing on a symbol is also very beautiful.

As a symbol we can use a yoni shaped crystal, a shell or even a papaya cut in half.

Yoni puja can be as elaborate or as simple as you want to make it. What matters most is your inner space and attitude of seeing the true essence of the yoni, and offering your love to that.

I encourage you to experiment with creating your own ritual in a way that speaks to your heart.

Here are some suggestions:

1. Start by preparing the physical space and transforming it into a sacred space. Use candles, beautiful fabrics, fragrant oils and flowers to set up the space.

2. Once everything is ready, we may utter some words expressing our devotion to the Universal mother and offer her prayers.

3. Then we move into the phase of silent contemplation — gazing at the yoni (or the symbol) with love, honor and reverence.

4. Make offerings to the yoni as a symbol of the Goddess or the Mother of the Universe. You may offer her candles, incense and flowers.

5. Stage five can be the ending meditation phase. Here we are silently contemplating the mystery of Shakti, the Divine mother.

6. You can conclude the ritual by taking a deep inhale together and making a long sound "haaa" on the exhale.

It is very important to keep the attitude of love and devotion towards Shakti, the Mother in all her forms throughout the entire ritual.

But let's get down to this important point: What is actually happening when the yoni is being worshipped?

What happens is that the Truth is coming back home. The yoni is seen for what she really is — pure Divinity. Everything is Divine, and yes, we can see the yoni as such. It is especially powerful to see the Divinity in the yoni and lingam. They are direct gateways to the Divine feminine and Divine masculine, respectively. We are perceiving this only to realize that we have never been separated.

I've had some pretty wild experiences each time I've received a yoni puja as well as every time I've held it for a group.

It is not at all uncommon to have flashes of past life memories streaming down your consciousness and other mystical experiences of remembrance and recognition.

17
Lingam as the Pillar of Consciousness

In India, in the beautiful city of Rishikesh there is a temple dedicate to Shiva lingam. The temple is a small room with a high ceiling and all that there is inside is a huge statue made of black marble. It is a statue of a huge and mighty cock. People come there every day to pray, to meditate and to perform an act of worship for the lingam.

Lingam is a beautiful word used in Tantra to speak about the penis. Literally, the word lingam means "the wand of light". The lingam is viewed as the representation of Shiva, of the pillar of the magnificent light of consciousness.

As I entered the temple, I felt a strong rush of energy up my spine. I came to my knees and bowed down in front of the lingam. Then I climbed the stairs and performed a lingam puja — a ritual of worship of the masculine essence. I was pouring milk, ghee and honey water on top of the lingam. Each of those liquids represent a quality of abundance, courage and love, and as I pour the liquids I am sanctifying these qualities and offering it all to pure consciousness, which is Shiva.

I spoke about how the tantric journey begins with self-love. We cannot authentically engage with the world and people around us unless we are in absolute acceptance and love of our own selves. Guess where self-love begins? It begins from our body. Because this is the part of ourselves that we see and deal with every single day. Our genitals are where our body begins. Our genitals are what determine our human essence our sexual essence. Our genitals need to be loved and acknowledged for what they are.

To me the cock is beautiful not only because I love the visual aspect of it, the sensation that it gives me when I touch it or when it's inside of me, but also because the cock is the direct link to the masculine consciousness. Most men don't really have a love for their cock, they are rather just using it either for pleasure or for giving pleasure.

I asked my lover once: *"What made you fall in love with your cock?"* He said: *"You."*

I was not surprised. I loved his cock. And I want to encourage all women to fall in love with the cock. Because we cannot truly love a man if we don't absolutely love the lingam.

Women can empower men to connect with their cock. But only when we have dealt with our own shame can we empower others. We are shaming others because of our own shame. We need to break out of this loop. We have no time for that, people! This is where the man begins. The cock is a representation of the Divine masculine.

The woman should honor the lingam of her lover as the **original Shiva lingam, the male principle.** This is the positive pole of the man. This is where man's power is. This is where a man is anchored. There are centuries of shame, and therefore, disconnect.

The mighty cock. How much I love thee.

I am with my lover, we are making out passionately. Then I place my hand on his lingam. Something incredible happens: I feel the energy from his cock entering into my hand and my arm, and it travels to my heart and amazing deep waves of devotion start flowing to me, and the most natural thing happens — I am worshipping his lingam, adoring him, praising him, bowing in front of the majesty that I see so clearly.

I feel so clear and open. That's why I can receive the might of what is in front of me, that cock, that lingam, the pillar of light.

Just seeing the reality, the absolute Divinity of what is front of me, brings me to my knees.

I start kissing him, touching him, taking him in my mouth. I am shaking in ecstasy. My kundalini starts rising and rising in waves and waves of devotion, and expansive orgasmic energy streaming and streaming through me, and overtakes me. I am orgasming from my throat, and my entire body. I cry and say that I adore the lingam, this is so beautiful.

For the man, it was quite an experience. He was not sure what was happening, but he knew that something profound, something Divine was going on.

A man's cock represents his sexual essence. It is his innermost essence in this human form. In fact, love for the lingam goes beyond the personality of this person or that. In this love, we accept and love the masculine essence of all. This love goes even beyond the cock of a particular man, but is love for the Cock himself.

Masculine essence begins with the physical sex organ, which is the lingam, and it expands into what the lingam represents — the stillness, pure presence that gives space to all. It is that container of vast, immeasurable consciousness that holds the space for all manifestation. Take a moment to feel into the greatness of this vision… This is called *transfiguration*.

Transfiguration is a special state of consciousness and practice of seeing the true essence of things. In Truth, all is Divine. If we remember that, if we work on raising our consciousness, we become big. Here is when we become capable of really loving. When our love is really that deep, it affects our entire being. It becomes so obvious, as if those three words are literally written on our faces: I love you.

And how do we feel around a person who truly loves our essence even without knowing us? We feel accepted. We feel seen. We feel honored. Of course, we are naturally attracted to that person.

And there is only one rule: transfiguration has to be real. It is not about imagining, or pretending that the human limitations don't exist. So my big invitation is to train yourself to see Divinity behind everything. Learn to recognize the beauty that permeates this existence.

Owning your cock

A big part of the journey for men is to start truly owning your cock. Generally, we live Life disconnected from our genitals. Even the expression "he thinks with his cock" is not really true. I actually wish that guys really were thinking more with their cocks!

Being in the lingam means being attuned to the body, rather than living life like a walking head. When men don't relax into their genitals, there is a tension. This tension brings discomfort that you naturally want to release. The most common solution that men refer to is quick masturbation to porn or sex that feels like masturbation inside of your partner followed by a peak orgasm with ejaculation. After that comes a relief. Until the tension builds up again. Then you want to release it again. So it becomes a continuous hassle of tension — release of tension. This is nothing but a shame-filled conditioned response to sexuality.

Instead, if there were no tension that needed to be released, you could access the power stored in your genitals continuously. You could drop into the space of your lingam, open up to your sexuality and relax into the erotic being that you are.

Here comes an important note, which may sound counter-intuitive. When you are accessing your sexuality in an ongoing way and are in a state of relaxation, you have less need to follow the pull of release. You don't have that unbearable itch in your genitals. You can come to the space of presence and make decisions from there. Hence, less interest in soul-less connections with others or simply wasting your sexual energy. Also, your erections will be stronger if you are owning your desire and your drive.

Exercise:

> *Stand up, feet shoulder width apart. Bend your knees slightly and place your hand over your groin. Bring all your awareness to this area. Direct your breath into your genitals. With every inhale, you are filling up your genitals with energy. You are dropping deeper. You are relaxing into your genitals, following the pull of gravity. You are beginning to occupy your genitals — to own them.*

Lingam Healing

A powerful way to heal the lingam and the owner's relationship to it is the practice of lingam massage.

There are many techniques of lingam massage, and it is great to experience these. Yet what is most important is that you establish a profound connection with your lingam.

It is great to massage and stretch your cock and balls daily.

Once the sensitivity of the lingam increases, men experience a wider range of sensation and orgasms.

A great thing to practice is slowing down and pausing both during self-pleasuring and during sex. Practice at times stopping completely yet staying erotically engaged and letting your cock do his job, without you needing to interfere.

I know it may sound really weird to some of you, my dear readers, yet I have to remind you that growth and transformation requires the courage to step out of the comfort zone, the paths that you have walked already, and being open to new ways, which may feel pretty awkward at first.

It makes a huge difference in the way you show up if you show up in full ownership of your cock.

Lingam Worship

Masculine essence begins with the physical sex organ, which is the lingam, and it expands into what the lingam represents — the stillness, pure presence that gives space to all. It is the container of the vast, immeasurable consciousness that holds the space for all the manifestation.

Feel into the greatness of this vision.

It is called transfiguration. Transfiguration is a special state of consciousness and practice of seeing the true essence of things.

In Truth, all is Divine.

Lingam puja helps the devotee reveal the light of consciousness that he is. The light of consciousness is the background for all creation.

According to Hindu tradition, the lingam puja takes the devotee step by step to Eternal Truth.
Lingam puja is a sacred tantric ritual dedicated to the worship of the masculine principle, as represented by the lingam. We express adoration for the Divine masculine principle.

This ritual originated in India, thousands of years ago. There are many various forms in which this ritual can be performed.

Just like the yoni puja, the ritual can be performed on a symbol, a sculpture or an object representing a lingam, or on a lingam in his living form.

A lingam puja can be an incredible gift that you can offer to your male partner or friend.

It is also incredibly healing both for the receiver and giver. The puja will purify and heal any mistrust in the masculine that you may have. It is also incredibly empowering for the man.

I encourage you to experiment with creating your own ritual in a way that speaks to your heart.

Here are the steps:

1. Start by preparing the physical space and transforming it into a sacred space. Use candles, beautiful fabrics, fragrant oils and flowers to set up the space.

2. Once everything is ready, utter some words expressing your devotion to the Divine masculine, to Shiva, the eternal light of consciousness.

3. Then move into the phase of silent contemplation — gazing upon the lingam with love, honor and reverence.

4. Make offerings to the lingam as the pillar of the light of consciousness. You may offer him candles, smoke of incense and flowers. You may praise him and sing to him.

5. Cleaning the lingam. In this stage, we are cooling down the lingam as by its nature it is full of heat. For this phase use water. After the cleaning, you may place flowers over the lingam.

6. Stage six is the ending meditation phase. Here we are resting in pure awareness. Allowing our hearts be seen and washed by the light of consciousness.

18
What sexual education failed to teach us.

Normally we get our *highly questionable* sexual education from pornography and from talking to friends about each other's sexual experiences. Pornography represents only 3% of what is possible in sexuality, but it is based on the masculine type of sexuality.

Now, there is nothing wrong with the masculine type of sexuality per se, but when it is cut off from the feminine type of sexuality a big imbalance is created.

The feminine system of arousal is very different from the male system of arousal.

Something that you've probably already understood as you've been reading this book is that our sexuality includes learnable skills.

Our body is an instrument. When we listen to it, it has a lot to teach us.

The mainstream model of sexuality is based on masculine arousal. Masculine and feminine sexuality is complimentary, yet they differ. What works for most men doesn't work for women, at least most of the time.

There are many women who think that their libido is very low, but in most cases, it is just the result of trying to have sex in a masculine way! Most of those women are trying to go into penetrative sex before they are fully aroused!

There is shockingly little awareness about it out there.

Generally speaking, male arousal is a yang type of arousal. The female type of arousal is a yin type of arousal.

What does that mean?

It means that **in the case of men** the sexual energy is like fire, it gets ignited in the center (the penis) and after that spreads out.

And **in the case of women**, the sexual energy is like water — it gets collected from the edges, the limbs and from the heart and then flows to the center (the vagina).

For men, their lingam can be touched without much foreplay. It is actually very nice to connect with the lingam first and

141

then continue by spreading the pleasure and activating his belly, chest and limbs.

For women, the yin energy proceeds from the edges gradually moving inward and flowing downward towards the sex center. The yin energy needs to pass through the heart center before it descends lower.

That's why women find it generally harder to separate sex from love. Most women need to feel connected and safe before they can open up. This is not always the case for men. They can have sex with someone without much emotional or heart connection.

Note: It all becomes more rich and complex when we have our masculine and feminine sides equally integrated!

The yoni and heart are similar — neither can be forced to open. You can't force yourself to fall in love, and you can't open your body by force.

So naturally it means that women take longer than men to get aroused.

But once you heat the water up, it can stay hot for a long time.

Also, the more frequently you bring her erotic energy to boil, the easier it will be to get her hot the next time.

Make sure that the woman is aroused before you touch her yoni. I cannot emphasize enough how important it is. I say this in every single training on feminine sexuality that I teach.

If you touch the yoni too soon, she will contract, freeze and close up.

Tantra is the tradition that honors and worships the Divine feminine. We can recognize the Divine feminine in all of Life, and in women in particularly.

Shakti flows more naturally through someone who is deeply in touch with the feminine. Usually it is women rather than men. (Although I know of some very remarkable men who are more in touch with their feminine than most women that I know.) Therefore, when the woman is fully aroused, **once all her body is loved and worshipped,** she will open her yoni. She will be fully orgasmic and she will share the nectar of the depth of her being with her partner. Then, the masculine partner will be able to ride her waves of pleasure.

It is a win-win situation!

Dear Men, please don't rush your woman into penetration. It does take presence and patience from you. If you offer her plenty of time to get deeply aroused and ecstatic before you penetrate her, it will come back to you tenfold.
When the entire system is activated, women can access amazing states of arousal and discover their deep erotic nature. Which they then share with their partner.

A note on pulling out

Many women have had the experience of not only being entered prematurely, but also being left prematurely.
This is relevant to intercourse, and other forms of intimacy, as well as to the closing of a relationship/separation, be it with

143

someone you spent only one night with or years together. It all ties in together and the mechanism is pretty much the same.

The best way to end the intercourse is to keep the genitals together, let the erection go down naturally, and still stay "plugged in" after the erection is gone. Then you will feel that the lingam naturally slides out of the yoni, or the woman will feel when she is ready to release him and she will gently push him out. This provides such a warm field of connection, nourishment and intimacy.

If the man has ejaculated don't let that be a reason to disconnect. I recommend that you keep your bodies close and the man covers the Yoni with his hand and holds her like that for a while. Wait until your bodies naturally feel ready to separate.

To sum up:

- Masculine sexual energy is like fire. It gets ignited in the center (the penis) and after that spreads out.
- Feminine sexual energy is like water. It gets collected from the edges, the limbs and from the heart and flows to the center (the vagina).
- If a woman's heart is soft and open, her yoni will be soft and open. None of these can be opened by force.
- The key to opening a woman's heart is to make sure her whole body is loved and worshipped.
- The lingam can be touched without much foreplay. It is actually very nice to connect with the

lingam first and then continue by spreading the pleasure and activating his chest, belly and limbs. This will facilitate full-body orgasms for the man.

• The deeper a woman's arousal is — the deeper the orgasms are. The deeper man's orgasms are, the more potential there is to enter into the infinite depth of the mystical union.

Exercise
Here are your guidelines for playing with the system of arousal:

Throughout your play you can try both — bouncing from man to woman, back and forth or start with fully activating the man, and then the woman and then the man again. As the woman will generally take longer to heat up (remember, she is like water), as she is arousing her beloved, she will be warming up as well (a little tip!)

To play with the man:

- Consciously connect with his lingam, caress, touch, kiss and lick it. Enjoy!
- Spend time exploring his testicles. Experiment with different types of touch — from barely touching with your fingertips to massaging them. You can try taking one testicle at a time or both together in your mouth. He will enjoy the warmth!
- Keep coming back to the lingam.
- Once you feel that his genitals are fully activated, start spreading the energy by moving your hands and attention throughout the rest

of his body. You can massage his legs and feet. Especially keep focusing on activating the space between his lingam and chest. In this way, his heart center will get activated.

- Follow your intuition. Be curious and playful! Now you can keep going back and forth from his chest, neck, face, lips and the rest of the body to his genitals.

To play with the woman:

- Make sure there is a lot of activation of her mouth, lips, neck, and most importantly, breasts.
- The way you approach her breasts also matters a lot. Explore every inch of her breasts before you even touch the nipple. The are lots of hidden erogenous zones. Every woman is actually capable of having breast-gasms!
- You can add elements of massage, and offer plenty of kisses to her shoulders, arms, legs, bum and hips. Offer gentle touch and kisses to her belly. Play with different types of touch — from feather-like touch to grasping and even slapping — expect surprises in her reaction!
- Then you can gradually make your way to her yoni. Start by exploring her pubic bone, vestibular bulbs (a VERY important erogenous zone as it is indirectly linked to the clitoris). Then touch the inner lips (make sure that whatever you touch them with is moist), only then, approach the clitoris.
- If you feel that she is inviting you into her yoni (by moving her hips and opening her legs more), don't hurry to go in, make her ask you!
- Note for the woman: when you are ready to be penetrated (either with a finger, tongue or lingam) — say it. Man, don't go in before that!

146

- If you think she forgot to ask you, you can ask: "Can I penetrate you now or would you prefer me to arouse you some more?" You'll be surprised at how much she is going to love this question, even if you have been together for many years.

- Follow your intuition. Be curious and playful!

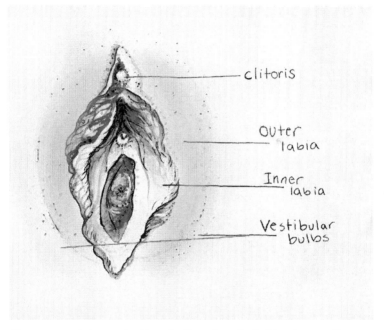

clitoris

outer labia

Inner labia

Vestibular bulbs

Once you go into penetration, don't go into the habitual way of having sex. Slow it down. And then, slow it down even more. Take pauses. Make it a meditative experience.

147

19
Self-pleasuring as an act of honoring yourself

I highly recommend you to self-pleasure, but not the way that most people know and are used to.

Normally, self-pleasuring is practiced with a fixation on an outcome. We stimulate ourselves with an agenda. An agenda being the goal to come to a specific type of orgasm. For most men, self-pleasuring will end with ejaculation, and for women with a peak orgasm. This will mark the end of the session after which we would carry on with the day.

This is not how I encourage you to practice it.

I encourage you to practice self-pleasuring as an act of self-love.

This is an act of taking the time to explore your body. You need to bring the attitude of curiosity to this process. Even if you have touched your body many times, there are many ways in which you can touch your body and there are so many various sensations that can open to you each time you touch yourself with full presence.

Drop expectations. Allow yourself to be surprised. This is huge.

Self-pleasuring is also an act of harnessing your sexual energy. You get to know your pleasure zones, and you even become more confident as a lover.

If you are a woman, you need to be guided by your anatomy of arousal. So you definitely want to activate your breasts first. Caress your shoulders, your limbs and only after that make your way to your yoni. And even after that — your yoni may not necessarily be open and willing for you to enter her. This is fine. You need to learn to listen to your yoni, and honor her desires. This is a profound way of healing, and developing a deep relationship with your center of power (which is your yoni). So if the yoni doesn't open and doesn't want to be entered, you need to honor that. But you don't need to stop self-pleasuring. You can explore the pubic bone as well as the outer labia that have a huge pleasure potential.

For a man, on the contrary, you can start by touching your lingam directly, but then you will be spreading the pleasure — moving it from the lingam and distributing it throughout your body. Remember the chapter about ejaculation — you will be bringing the same attitude to your self-pleasuring session.

Find a safe space and time to explore your body. Stimulate yourself in whatever way you like to create the most arousal. When you arrive at the edge of your pleasure, just before the point of no return, deepen your breath, slow down and become aware of yourself at that edge. Try to ride your edge without going over it.

If you "have an accident" — that's what some tantric men call it when they ejaculate without a conscious choice to do so — stay present with your sensations and enjoy.

Eventually, you will learn to stop before you reach the point of no return. Consistent daily practice is key. In this case practice means penetrative sex or self-pleasuring.

It's important to remember that this type of self pleasure practice is completely different from what you are used to doing. It is going to take some time unlearning the old ways.

As a result of this practice, you will be able to ride orgasmic waves of pleasure that are way deeper than what an even the most amazing ejaculatory orgasm offers you.

We tend to treat the body like an object, even the way we touch our own bodies is much like touching a table. We tend to enter the body from the outside.

In fact, we need to enter the body from the inside.

When we are performing the act of conscious self-pleasuring, the aim is not to come to a peak experience or orgasmic release, but to take the time to explore our genitals, our whole body, to activate it, to drop in.

Through presence, always through presence, we are dropping in; we are getting to know our own selves.

Only then will we find out that our genitals have stories to tell us and information to pass along.

It is essential for a healthy relationship with your sexuality to touch your genitals with love and reverence every single day, no matter if you are in a relationship or not, but especially if you are not in a relationship or not having regular sex. You need to be accessing our sexual energy in an ongoing way. This will allow you to be more productive in Life and manifest the Life that you desire without much effort.

Sexual energy is the core energy of our being. This is the energy that manifests and creates.

As you are performing self-pleasuring, use all of your body, with every breath drop deeper into your body. Don't let your mind take over and indulge in fantasies or remembering past experiences. This doesn't mean that it is never ok to fantasize. But mostly you need to train yourself to switch off your mind and be with your experience. Most of our sex life is happening in the mind, but you don't want to be a slave to that. You want to explore the pleasure potential that's contained in your own body. Thus using this as a gateway to deeper self-love.

On my website **www.sofiasundari.com** you can download guided self pleasure practices.

Love of the body is where self-love should start because if we are constantly unhappy with our own body we cannot fully love ourselves. By judging it we create big blockages for ourselves. We need not only to come to peace with the way our body looks and feels, but we need to fall in love with all of it as the expression of our Self.

Then, you release the need for others to love your body. This is when your whole flavor will change. It will change from that of someone who needs to be loved and acknowledged to someone who is complete in their own self-love, and doesn't need to be stimulated by the love of someone else.

It's great to feel someone else's love, but it doesn't need to come from a place of neediness – because you don't have enough of your own love. It can come from a place of desire to expand, enjoy, share and celebrate together.

In this way, your being becomes infused by the nectar of love.

20
Owning your Intensity

Your own intensity. Your sexual power. What is it like? Can you feel it in your pussy? Can you feel it in your veins running in the heat of your blood? Can you feel it in your cock?

This is your fire.

Maybe you've had a glimpse... It is worth totally diving into it; allowing yourself to feel the parts of you that can do anything. The parts that can tell a stranger that you want to have sex with them. That can interfere in a street fight. That can express your own truth and stand for it with all your might. That can jump from a 10-meter-high cliff into ice-cold water.

Your intensity is wild. Your intensity is magnificent. Your intensity is intimidating for many, many reasons.

But the main question is: Is your own intensity intimidating you?

Most probably it is. Most probably, you put a bunch of stuff into a box with a big black label "dirty". You chose not to look into that box ever again — or only in secret, when no one can see you. After looking in it, you do anything you can to forget you saw it.

But there is something that fascinates you about it. There is something in that darkness. Something juicy. Something scary. Something that feels big. And I'll tell you what it is. My darling, it is your light. It may be disguised as darkness. And feel so scary. But as you go right into it, as you simply make a choice to be with it. Once you stop judging it, once you start owning it… you will be amazed.

Not only will you feel at peace with your own self, and leave the nightmare of needing to suppress yourself. But you will also have a different resonance and will be attracting people who can be with your intensity, your brightness and your magnificent beauty.

Have you ever felt that you need to be taken now and that's the only thing that matters? Have you ever felt that you are addicted to sex, and you only want more and more of this sweet medicine?
Have you ever felt trembling in your womb that feels like an erupting volcano?
Have you ever felt your yoni yearning to be filled?
Have you ever felt the depth of all that?
Have you ever felt the depth of your sexual desire?

We all live in the world where **sexuality is generally not accepted.** There is a lot of conditioning that makes many people believe that sexuality is dirty, and we all carry a degree of shame around it.

For me, it was almost shocking to realize recently that even after years of expanding and taking ownership of my sexuality, I could still find some good old shame there. This feeling of shame normally comes in a package with our childhood. I spoke a lot about it in the beginning of this book.

Eve Ensler in her book *The Vagina Monologues* shares a story of an old woman who at a younger age was making out with a boy and got so aroused that her juices started flowing abundantly. The boy had no clue in regards to what was happening and told her off, saying that she was "a weird stinky girl". This ignorance resulted in a massive traumatic experience for that woman and since then, she not only never dared to engage with men, but also never even touched or thought about her vagina. How insane is that? Such abundant lubrication and amrita of a woman is a profound gift. That woman was actually having a mystical experience and it shows how sexually open she was. We would make a mistake if we were to blame the boy. The boy had no clue about this aspect of sexuality and spirituality, just lots of shame like 95% of people on this planet.

Maybe you have felt that dense deep sexual energy, sometimes it may feel heavy like a weight at the level of your base chakra, other times — like bubbling champagne that spreads all the way along your spine and perhaps your entire body. Maybe it has been disturbing at times — say you need to work or study, but all you can think of is sex. Maybe you felt it was a problem and it was not spiritual to feel horny all the time. Well, let me tell you something.

If you can relate to anything that you read above, you are blessed.

You are blessed because you have experienced your sexual energy, meaning it is not blocked or not entirely blocked. Everyone has it, but very little approve of it. This sexual energy is a gift. This sexual energy is the energy of Life itself. And it is deeply spiritual. Here's why.

It is my experience and observation that only sexually open people are able to experience deep levels of devotion, of yearning for the Divine.

If there is a reason for our feeling of separation from our own Divinity, the feeling of intense fiery devotion then, love is the most beautiful one.

To be able to love and to be devotional, our energetic body needs to be awakened. We need to know what eroticism feels like, what it feels like to desire deeply, to be sexual, to be in the body. We need to know what it feels like to be fully alive.

Let me remind you: **our sexuality is not dependent on whether we are in a relationship or not,** or whether we have sex or not, it's not about feeling "sexy". An erotically awake person can always be sexual; it does not depend on the external circumstances.

Now, sometimes it happens that very sexual people may feel a lack of libido. It has definitely happened to me. And it is absolutely natural to have phases of not feeling sexual at all. But if you find yourself stuck in this non-sexual phase, feeling turned off and uninspired… here it boils down to something very simple: a choice.

It is up to us if we want to feel alive or numb. If we want to feel erotically alive or stuck in our heads, questioning and resisting.

It's true that some might need to do more work to get there than others. Here is some great news for you — it's really not that difficult, because it is our natural state. Remember, first of all it is choice. It's a choice to keep holding onto the shame and the wounds of our past. It is a choice to be stuck in our judgment and envy of other people's sexual expression. Normally, these two are closely interlinked. Sometimes, we are also conditioned to feel guilty for our desire, but this only happens because we don't see it as sacred. We haven't yet felt the very depth of it.

When you feel sexual desire try sitting with it, close your eyes and feel it in your body. It may start off with a fantasy or just the anticipation of something yummy that's going to happen. Stay focused on the feeling. Where in your body can you feel this wanting? Stay with it. There might be a need that wants to be fulfilled. Feel deeper. Feel so deep, no thoughts move. **Feel deeper and deeper until you reach all the way to your most profound longing.**

This longing is pure. This longing is what powers all manifestation. This longing is for the Divine. And it is endlessly beautiful.

When we feel so deeply we are empowered. Empowered to live fully, to shine brightly, to enjoy Life, and to inspire everyone around us. Owning our sexuality expands us like nothing else. Owning our sexuality is the game changer.

And there can never be too much of a good thing.

21
Opening as a Soul Force.
Opening as a Response to Life.

Have you ever observed your reaction to intensity?

I am referring to intensity of strong emotions (your own or someone else's) or of the sharp sensation of pain or discomfort.

The habitual response to intensity is protection.

Usually protection manifests in one of the three ways:
1. You get angry and loud (subconsciously trying to throw off the energy),
2. You withdraw, become cold and hard,
3. You look cool as if you are not reacting, but in fact, you are suppressing the emotion.

It is the same with orgasm. Sexual energy has a lot of intensity. Habitually, we are protecting ourselves from feeling the fullness of it. It may be hard to believe, but it's true. That's why so few people have ever experienced those profound life-changing earth-shaking soul-moving orgasms.

Observe how you relate to water.

The water element is the element directly linked with the second chakra and thus, with our sexuality.

Therefore, the way we relate to water is symbolic of the way we relate to our sexuality and emotions.

Observe how do you react when you enterinto cold water. Do you come in with a sense of ease and relaxation, or do you contract and tense up? This is very symbolic to how you respond to intensity.

It is possible to enter into cold water, as well as intense sensations, and wild emotions with a sense of ease and relaxation. We can re-program ourselves and see each sensation as a gateway to pleasure. Including the intense and uncomfortable ones.

In Tantra, we work a lot with elements of nature, and we can learn from the elements. Water is the element that teaches us how to flow.

The key is opening.

Opening despite all the programming that is making you close off. Opening despite the fear of the unknown (because it is way out of your comfort zone). When you first start opening instead of closing *it may hurt like hell.*

It will hurt because when you choose to open, the hurt that has accumulated behind the protective shield suddenly comes back to the surface. Every human being's heart has been closed for centuries by layers and layers of hurt, and by coping with each hurt by closing a little bit more.

So you have a choice to make: Will you keep closing, or will you dare to stay with the pain?

If you let yourself feel just a little bit of the pain and stay with it, feel it, open to it — it gets released. Once a feeling is fully felt, the tension around it vanishes.

When you train yourself to open to everything that comes, you can have a "clean as you go" policy, so nothing gets accumulated, but rather, you feel all emotions as they come and let the tension go.

The more you practice it, the easier it gets. Eventually, nothing will stick to you.

When we are opening to everything instead of closing, what we are actually doing is opening to love.

Love is not meant to look a specific way.

Each time you chose opening instead of closing, you are making yourself more available to love. If you are happy – open more. If you are sad – open more. If you are confused – open more. And even if you are hurt – open more.
I can't emphasize enough how big this is. If you are able to stay open and open more in the toughest times you

161

become empowered, wise and so deep. Your little ego will be screaming: "Are you crazy! This is too much. Where is your pride!?" And if you can still open the result will blow your mind.

When H. and I first met, we wanted two different things. He wanted to be open and explore, and I wanted only him, to get married, and make babies.

That first year was a hell of a ride. With me pleasing, swearing, crying, yelling, proving, doing anything I could to make him fully choose me and only me. And again and again I would get burnt by his fire. That fire didn't want to settle. And that fire was burning holes in my ego.

Through those holes I could finally see God.

It was the first time in my life when the amount of pain opened me to a profound realisation that I could not hold onto anything but the divine. **That blasted me open. The heat of devotion took over. I started seeing the divine in everything. It became really wild.**

At some point he showed up after a prolonged meditation retreat and told me that he didn't love anyone, didn't love me, didn't love himself… He was cold, and it was really painful. But I decided to do something I had never done before – I decided to keep opening, even through his closing. Even when we were making love he was cold and distant and I would end

162

up in tears, but I kept opening. I kept on and on. I put all my willpower into staying open no matter what he was doing or saying. It went on for weeks, and when I couldn't take it anymore and decided to give up... he opened up.

There are two levels of Opening:

- Energetic opening (may include physical)
- Opening of the heart/consciousness

Both are required for orgasms. You need to totally surrender your body, you let go of any clenching, plus open your mind, your heart and your consciousness.

It is always good to practice staying open at the level of your heart/consciousness. It can actually become your day-to-day practice.

For example, when someone talks to you, respond with openness. This is very powerful in arguments: instead of being defensive and ready to reflect the attack. These are powerful opportunities to open: you stop the toxic exchange and the tension just like that.

More on opening of the heart/consciousness read Chapter 11 – Keys to developing full body orgasms.

When it comes to energetic opening, you don't always want that, especially in public places or situations where you feel unsafe, or when you don't want to be approached.

Therefore, we can learn to seal our energy and affirm our boundaries.

Setting up Energetic Boundaries

Energetic opening makes you very vulnerable. It is great for intimacy and sexuality, because the more you allow yourself to be vulnerable, the deeper your orgasm will be.

Yet, I am not saying that you need to be energetically open at all times.

Energetic opening makes you very available, but you do not always want that. You don't want to be available for toxic energy.

As your energy becomes intelligent, you can also learn to seal it.

It starts from clarity: you need to be clear with yourself about what you want to be open for and what you don't.

> *I once was dating a very handsome man; actually, all the men I have dated have been exceptionally handsome. But that particular one was incredibly alluring to most women. It was fascinating to observe that wherever he would show up, he would end up being surrounded by women. Women would constantly fall for him or sometimes, a friendly hug from his side would excite a*

woman so much she would literally start orgasming in his arms.

Of course, to a large degree it was the result of his physical attractiveness. Yet, I could see that there was more to it. His energy was incredibly open and available at all times, and this looked and felt like an invitation.

There is nothing wrong with that as long as he is choosing this kind of interaction. Yet, he shared with me that he had no idea why these women were sticking to him, because he had no interest in any of them.

His energy was wide open at all times. So I invited him to acknowledge that. And tune into whether he really didn't want to give an impression of such availability. We could see that there were parts of him that actually liked it a lot — they were getting validation from that.

Wherever you are in the process, the first step is to come to clarity: Do you want your energy to be wide open or not?

Sometimes it will be yes, other times, no. This is how you learn your boundaries.

Some examples of circumstances when you definitely don't want to have your energy wide open: hospitals, public bathrooms, public events with lots of wild and crazy energy, public transport and times when you just don't want to interact.

Once you have come to clarity, and you know that it is time to seal your energy, do the following:

Bring your awareness to your manipura chakra (in the Chinese tradition it is known as *dantian* and in the Japanese, *hara*.), you can also place your both hands over this point and breathe into your belly.

On top of that, you can add breathing with throat friction or *ujjayi breath* (you might be familiar with it from yoga —it involves contracting the throat, which creates a hissing sound on the inhale and exhale), and direct your breath to your belly. This will make your energetic body more dense and seal it nicely. Keep your awareness there until you are in a place where you can fully open.

Dantian

22
Become the Magnificent Lover You Are

To me there are not many things in Life that are as empowering as a lover who fully embraces my sexual expression. It takes a lover who is sexually free him/herself. Who has dealt with the social conditioning and shame around their own sexuality.

Growing up, we all received messages that we need to hold back, that we shouldn't show how much we are attracted to someone, that we need to be reserved, and wait until the man makes the move. This is especially true for women. Even being among people who are quite open sexually, I received messages that I needed to somehow hide my sexuality, that it was bad if someone saw me naked, that I should be a bit less loud, a bit less expressive and desire less. All these messages, sometimes subtle, sometimes very loud are coming from a shamed and conditioned place within the people who are sending these messages out.

It is incredibly liberating and empowering to be with a

167

lover who accepts your sexuality fully, who encourages you to be always more of what you are, and never, less. These lovers become our light workers, our most intimate healers. They help us heal any remaining shame around our sexual expression. These lovers are the lovers of God within us. And these lovers will save the world.

Once we feel that there is no need to hold back, once we fully accept our sexual insatiable nature, once we are free to express our desire, a vast space opens up. Suddenly, sexuality stops being something done only behind closed curtains. Sexuality becomes what it truly is — a powerful force, an expression of deep intimacy, a natural expression of our essence. We suddenly become real. We suddenly become Divine.

To my Divine lover:

> *"I want to melt into you. I want to fully surrender to you. I offer you my heart. I offer you my yoni. I give myself to you, completely... I desire you. I desire God in you. I can't help but fantasize about your gorgeous hands on my naked body. I cannot help but dream of your tongue gently touching my lips and then making its way into my mouth with passion. I cannot help but feel my yoni opening, imagining your naked body against mine. I cannot help but fantasize about your lingam and that unique chemistry that happens when our two bodies unite. Tenderness and edge. Softness with a warning. Masks drop before we know it. Fears, inhibitions, insecurities vanish into fire. Simply thinking of you makes me melt.*
>
> *I want to feel you from the inside."*

A note on the feminine and the masculine

Each of us is a deep multifaceted being. Regardless of gender we all have feminine and masculine sides. The feminine in us is that part of us that flows, that feels, that is emotional and that longs for connection. Ultimately the feminine is Shakti, she is Life. The masculine in us is the part of us that is directed, goal oriented and driven. Ultimately the masculine is Shiva, nothingness. Achieving goals gives him the sense of completion that he is longing for, so he can finally be empty. It is important that we develop both: our inner man and inner woman. When we have a healthy relationship between our inner masculine and inner feminine, we no longer need to engage in relationships with others to get a sense of completeness, because we have it within ourselves.
Sexually speaking, it is great to develop both: the ability to penetrate (be it with the lingam or energetically) and the openness to be penetrated. Although generally we will be happier in one of these roles, depending on the nature of our sexual essence.

So let's look at the deepest desires of the masculine and feminine.

Below I am making a general assumption that women carry a feminine sexual essence, and men – masculine. However, it may very well be reverse.

What Does the Feminine Want?

Women… they will feed you with their "I don't know" and
"Maybe"…
Women… will confuse you with their changing mind…
Women… will make you feel like you are losing your ground…

They will test you, drive you nuts, encourage you, discourage
you, blow you open, shut you down, demand attention, bitch
around, come with an earth-shaking gift. But women will
rarely tell you what they want. Not because we want to
hide it, but because our deepest desire of the feminine is not
intellectual.

Deep down the feminine wants one thing. She wants your
depth. She wants your truth. She wants to feel penetrated. And
not only by your lingam. She wants to feel penetrated by your
energy, by your love, by your presence, by your consciousness.
She wants to feel that consciousness/Shiva touches every
single secret spot within her.

The feminine yearns to be seen. That's where all the makeup,
fancy dresses and obsession with our body parts come from.
All that merely mimics the real yearning to be seen deeply, to
be met, to feel entered all the way to the level of our soul.

She wants to feel your consciousness deep inside of her. She
longs to surrender, to open up beyond measure. She wants the
real you. She wants to feel your edge. She wants you to not be
intimidated by your own desire. She wants to feel you owning
your cock. Actually, on a very practical note, something really
powerful that a man can do in or outside of lovemaking is
energetically "drop" into his cock.

Be present with your partner, look into each other's eyes and at the same time, feel into your lingam, and visualize/ feel how you are dropping into it. Eventually, you will feel as if your lingam becomes energetically bigger. You give him space. And if your partner is sensitive enough, just that may trigger a massive orgasmic wave of pleasure in her. Because she wants to feel all of you. And she cannot feel you when you are stuck in your mind. When you are fully in your cock — you are fully in your male power. There's not much that you have to do from there. Start by just being.

In the being, we will meet. From there you will know.

Beloved Shiva,
My desire for you is endless.
My desire for you is beyond what I can describe.
I want to receive you completely.
I want to honor and worship you until I exist.
I'm on my knees before you forever.

Sometimes I will show up very sweet and beautiful,
Other times — glorious and wise,
Or — passionate and blissful,
Or — intense, too much, too emotional, too loud, too expressive,
Or — so humble and quiet like a lake...

And I beg you,
Please Beloved
Don't try to handle me,
Don't try to fix me,
Don't tell me what to do,

171

Don't give me direction,
Don't try to fulfill or satisfy me,
Don't try to impress me,
Don't try to understand me...

Beloved,
I want only one thing from you:
Your complete and undivided presence.
For that, you only need to be here, without agenda.
This is the greatest gift you can ever give me.
In that space I can BE.
Be fully. Be my bliss. Be my rawness. Be all that I am.
Be fully seen.
Feel fully loved.

What Does the Masculine Want?

We cannot really separate sexuality from Life, that's why to understand what men want from women in bed, we need to understand what they want from women in general.

I have come to realize that in their hearts all men deeply want to see women happy. I've observed that when women need something and ask: "Can you help me?" They will answer: "Yes, how?" Or: "Can you do something for me?" The answer is often: "Yes, what?"

Even if the task is very difficult for the man, if it is very clear what exactly a woman needs, most men will do anything possible to make that happen. Often we simply need to allow them to do it. And let them feel empowered by it. It is empowering to feel that what we have to offer is received.

In times of intensity, I witness myself reaching out to the masculine for support and protection.

> *September 2015. After a fight with my brother, I'm crying and yelling in the middle of a busy street in Moscow. I am overtaken by my emotions, I am a total mess, I cannot put myself together. Suddenly I follow my instinct - I reach for my phone to call my dad. He picks up immediately and my extreme feminine energy (wild emotions, strong energy) in that moment places him deep into his masculine. It is hard to understand what I am saying because I am being choked by my own tears. Yet, he is embodying pure consciousness and straightens me up with utmost confidence and calmness. He says a few very simple logical things and gives me step by step instruction of what I should do. This calms me down in no time.*
>
> *I'm in awe. I open up. Deep gratitude.*

I am constantly touched by the men around me, by their deep care and support. I find it incredibly beautiful that the masculine accepts every offer to show up and be the hero for the feminine, when the feminine really welcomes and allows it.

Generally, women don't express enough appreciation for men. We tend to take things for granted and not acknowledge them for the magnificent warriors that they really are. Or, we just think that it is so obvious that we appreciate them that there is no need to express it. Yet, it is so important for them to feel that acknowledgement, that validation by the feminine; to hear about even the tiniest things that contribute to our happiness.

Each man wants to be a hero. When he doesn't believe he is, he feels emasculated.

To every man reading these words I want to say: I appreciate your presence so deeply. I am cheering you on every time you don't give up, when you show your heart and your courage, when you go for things that actually scare you. I love how deep in your hearts you just want to see women happy. I love the deep masculine essence of every man.

I asked several men who I respect very much what they want from a woman. Here are a few answers that touched me most:

> *"First of all, I want for a woman to feel, to be, to act and to trust in her own empowered self, every woman and every girl. This is my wish, that all is blessed in our world, that women feel safe and honored. I want my woman to be able to trust to the point of being totally open to receive the depths of my passion, to surrender to a no-destination threshold where everything is possible and all expectations are created moment by moment. I want her to be brutally honest and to be able to receive the same and for both of us to understand that it's a reflection of action and not a finite mandate.*

> *I have developed a dear, dear relationship with all my sisters in these past three years once I stopped seeing them as potential somethings and truly met them at a level of sisterhood seeing them as my daughters, my mothers, my sisters and ultimately, my most trusted council.*

> *There has been lots of shedding of old predatory*

*masculine sexual energy and dominant programming
that I have consciously been focusing on shifting out of
my operating system so that I can clearly be a present
and honoring man, brother and father in this world." -*
Keith

*"Beyond all the wants, if you ask most men whether they
choose to have purpose and peace in their life, most would
say yes. Both of these you can offer a man, but it will
never satiate a man. You can never give a man what he
wants. So forget about it! It must be something he finds
within himself, in his own time and with the freedom
to do so. There are ways to empower him to come to this
place on his own. I will offer you some suggestions on
how to do this.*

*Listen to your body and receive the answers you seek.
Share those answers with the man you are with or wish
to attract, without projection. If fear or emotions arise,
own them, love them and express them. Give him the
opportunity to serve you in that vulnerability, no matter
where he is or how he is showing up for you. Gift him
with your vulnerability. This gives him purpose within
the connection you share together. This gifts him with the
beauty of the feminine softness. He wants to be present to
this. In this, he can offer his gifts.*

*Men love feeling a sense of purpose. When they feel
they have purpose and can offer the gifts that they feel
confident in giving, it gives them a sense of direction
and meaning to their life and in their relationship with
you. Tell them how to serve you in your vulnerability*

without force. Just offer them a way to serve you that feels right for you. They then can rest/find peace in knowing they have been present with themselves and to you in this existence. They have been present, given their gift, and when that gift is received, they find peace. Receive the gifts he has to offer and encourage and nurture his growth on his road to finding peace within. One day he will find purpose and peace in just existing. Just being." - Deva

"I want my woman to feel safe with me so she can open. Presence. I want her to tell me what she wants. I want her feedback in the form of words or gestures. I want her to be wild, aggressive, sensual, soft and hard. I want to be adored and worshipped. I want her to initiate. I want her to use her whole being.

I want her to experiment. And I want her to be empowered and lovingly taking care of her body." - Dominik

23
Surrender Is Not Scary.
Surrender Is the Only Way

*Do you want to change the world? Then love. With all
your heart, love.*

To the mind, the idea of surrender may sound weird. Even
silly. Even scary. The mind will never understand what
surrender really is. Our little ego is very good at creating walls
of protection, but incapable of love.

The mind is good at setting up boundaries, claiming our
territory. But surrender is a word from another realm — from
the realm of the heart.

We can work around explaining surrender, and we can
understand the beauty of the concept. Yet, it is something that
can only be experienced in the heart.

Everyone is afraid of the melting, of losing ourselves. It is
only the mind that's scared to get overwhelmed. And not in
vain! The mind gets overwhelmed easily.

177

In fact, surrender is the only way to find our Self. The only parts of us that can burn away are the false ones. The paradox is that the deeper we surrender, the stronger we become. We melt into a completely different view of ourselves, and with a lot of love that can defeat anything.

There is no greater safety than being wrapped in the arms of Divinity.

We can let love be our teacher, our guide. We can choose love as our path. This is what we are surrendering to. In surrender, we are always surrendering to love. And love is but another name for God.

This path is not for everyone. Only the courageous ones can walk it. It is not always going to be a pleasant ride. Sometimes, you will be devastated. Sometimes, your own mind will be sending you terrible demons. Sometimes, you will want to close off and disconnect from all feelings.

And then, you will remember… millennia of being disconnected. Millennia of a world ruled by the mind. This disconnect is not personal, it is collective. And we all know it and feel it acutely.

You will see that you don't know what is right and what is wrong. But if you have felt your heart, if you have allowed yourself to love, even if only a little bit of it… If you have tasted the nectar, there is no way back.

It is a one-way road. And it is the most glorious one: the road of love.

We should never surrender to another person. When we do that, we inevitably feel hurt and betrayed. We should only ever surrender to the Divine. Surrendering to the Divine within ourselves and within the Beloved is an incredibly beautiful way to live.

Surrender is not submissiveness. Submissiveness is either an unconscious manipulation strategy or something that is coming from a place of feeling like a victim of a situation.

Surrender is not weak. Yes, it makes us very vulnerable, very open. Vulnerability is what makes all the difference. It's what makes life worth living, what brings meaning, what brings purpose. Vulnerability is the source of joy, real creativity, belonging and love. But, it is not weak. On the contrary, it is something that makes us invincible. It may sound paradoxical to you, but when you truly deeply surrender, nothing can really hurt you. When you truly surrender, you become vast like the ocean. You become spacious. You become big. Things may come and touch you, yet they won't stick to you. Because when you are so vast, there is nothing to stick to.

Vulnerability is right here,
In not knowing if you are going to get a response after you say "I love you",
In breathing through shame, grief and insecurities,
In showing up in the most uncomfortable places,
In asking for help when all you want is close your eyes and run,
In choosing opening even when no-one else responds with opening,
In living without a safety net,

In saying yes to the uncertainty,
In trusting the illogical, the unknown,
In choosing to love with our whole heart even when there
is no guarantee that the other will open in response,
In healing the world through openness of love.
Vulnerability is right here,
beneath millennia of numbness and disconnect.
When vulnerability is a choice it doesn't make us weak.
It becomes an enlightened vulnerability.
Enlightened vulnerability is invincible.
It does take a lot of heart and willingness to show up
unpolished, vulnerable, raw.
But that's what makes this life worth living.

Surrender is also the key for deep pleasure, expansiveness and orgasms.

In fact, without surrender we cannot orgasm.

The deeper your surrender, the more you give yourself to the sensations, to the energy, to the pleasure, the more likely you are to lose yourself in the trance of deep pleasure.

Surrender comes hand in hand with trust.

A lover told me once: *"There are many things I admire about you, but what turns me on the most is your trust."*

Trust can take many shapes. It can look like self-confidence. It can look like integrity. It can look like dignity. But real meaning of trust is deeper.

Real trust is about opening to Life. It is about loving Life. Having a deep vision of this reality. Acknowledging depth in everything and everyone. Remembering the deep meaning of this Life. Trusting that all is guided by the Great One.

In trust, we offer ourselves to each moment in totality, like we would to the most magnificent lover. A lover that is intense and knows what s/he wants, that pushes your limits and takes you out of your comfort zone. And yet, you trust your lover, because you also feel how much s/he honors you.

Let Life be that lover. Let Life be a work of art that your mind never could have created. It can only be a work of art when we give ourselves completely, fully, without holding back. It's not that we give ourselves to something or someone specific. We give ourselves to everything — and to nothing. We give ourselves back to ourselves.

I have discovered my sacred assignment.
My assignment is to love.
To love so deeply I cannot hear the rants of my mind.
To love so deeply I act with absolute certainty, though
I may not have the slightest idea what I will do next. I
know nothing but the deep certainty of love, and how it
wants to be expressed in this present moment.

In this surrender, I allow everything to arise, and I feel
into its depth. I open as everything. I open as the entire
cosmos.

And from there I begin my holy work.

181

24
Orgasm into Liberation

The endless beauty of losing yourself

Tantra is a paradox. At times you will find the teachings very confusing —for the mind.

But the truth is, in Tantra we don't want to stay at the level of the mind, we keep pressing deeper, we keep going beyond the mind.

But that's just at the surface. The truth is that in Tantra, we don't want to stay at the level of the mind: we want to keep pressing deeper, to keep going… deeper, farther, beyond the mind.

That's why you may hear me say one thing today, and tomorrow I may say something completely the opposite. The amazing thing is that both will be true.

Looking at the larger picture, we move through three stages in developing our sexuality and orgasmic-ness.

Stage 1: the *Ice Queen/Ice King*. We are covered in ice; we're numb. In this stage, our behavior is unconscious as we try to figure out Life. We experience this stage as being stuck in the expectations of the outer world—feeling like things happen to us, and blaming the world when our expectations are not met.

Stage 2: the *Wild Woman/Man*. We come into our own, growing in autonomy, strength and authenticity. In this stage, we feel empowered: we stand tall and strong by ourselves, no matter whether we have a partner or not.

You own your pleasure. You own your intensity. And *you* are a complete human being. In the wild woman/man stage, you dare to question any beliefs or dogmas present in society, and you relate to others from this place.

To those in the first stage, you may seem indifferent, "too detached" or distant. In fact, you are simply clear—rooted in your own Self, which is a very important place for human beings to come to. This is the place of empowerment, where you can enter into an "H-type" relationship, one in which two individuals stand tall and strong, even though there is a link between them and they choose to cultivate their connection. They do not meet from a place of neediness, as in the first stage. They meet from a place of wanting to be with someone and of sharing their depth. They just *are*: growing together, they see what the alchemy between them can bring.

Stage 3: the *Priest/Priestess*. The third stage is about dropping all of that. In the third stage, you've already done so much

183

work that you are completely present and have expanded your consciousness. You feel you are giving fully. You are in the flow of Life.

This is when everything has been dropped: everything you've ever known, even your empowerment—even that individuality in which you used to stand so tall and strong. Even the idea of being rooted in anything. At this stage, you willingly let yourself get lost. Completely lost.

Here, you stop being concerned about sealing your energy or protecting yourself from external influences.

This is what we experience as full orgasm, as orgasmic living.

If at some point, you discover that you've forgotten your own name or where in the world you are, that's great. It means you are opening/have opened into real orgasm. Here, you forget about your "little me" and its precious identity that needs to be centered and even present. Here, you let go of control and surrender fully.

Now, if you look at this from the standpoint of someone in the first stage, this is horrible! It doesn't make any sense.

From the second stage, it looks pretty scary. You may think to yourself, *What if something bad happens? What if someone takes advantage of me? What if I get used or I pick up some bad energy?*

Yet it is only from the third stage that we can comprehend.

The third stage is pure heart. You release yourself from the neediness of the mind. You drop into pure heart space.

The heart has no doubts, no worries, no fears. The heart's nature is to be open. Opening is all the heart wants. And continually opening is what matters the most, because this is how you drop back into the Universal Heart.

In orgasm, a state arrives when you have to drop everything: you, me, the objects around us, our neighbors, location, nation, time. This state is when your true essence can blossom. This state is when the separation between the masculine and the feminine stops making sense, when we go beyond concepts.

In this state, you expand into the galaxy.

***

"I am here in Hawaii, finding myself in a warm spring water pool by the ocean. My legs are wrapped around my lover's waist; his lingam is inside me. I lean backwards. I feel the warmth of the water, embracing me, caressing me tenderly... I give myself fully to the water. I offer my body to the experience of this moment... I am turned on by my body's ability to experience nature so deeply. This is incredibly erotic.

My lover is here, holding my lower back. I feel his presence... It helps me drop even deeper. He starts thrusting inside of me slowly. I feel my body rocking, which stimulates the waves of pleasure. I feel kundalini starting to shake my body. There is nothing for me to

185

do except surrender to the ecstasy spreading through my entire body. I moan quietly.

This continues for a little while.

Then the sound stops. The space opens up: something bigger is happening. My lover feels it too and becomes still. My breathing stops. I cannot experience my limits. I feel met by the ocean. I am as big as the ocean. My body is the water. The water is me.

Time stops. I am free."

***

Once we have found our path—one we have chosen and are committed to— there comes a time when we realize that it is a one-way street. We have attracted the attention of our Higher Self, of our Spirit.

From that point on, all that doesn't serve us starts falling away by itself. We turn into the best possible version of ourselves with every step. We stretch. We are being worked on. We grow—at times through pain, only to realize that it has only been the pain of birthing ourselves. We are becoming vaster, bigger. Our consciousness rises. All this happens so that we can give more and truly serve love. So that we can be the instrument of Divine love.

It is very important to hold this vision, because even the most beautiful things get polluted when taken out of the context of why we do them.

The mere fact that you are reading these words isn't something to take for granted. The majority of this world lives in sheer ignorance. If you have access to knowledge and information—that is very special. If you have access to this sacred path—it is a privilege. This knowledge and this access is not given to someone who is not ready for it. What we choose to do with it is what matters.

No matter what practice you move into and what choice you make, always remember the why. Consecrate your actions to the benefit of all. Eject yourself from this ego-driven life, expand your vision and embody the vastness of consciousness.

It's not too difficult. It's not scary.

You were born for this.

***

Here we are at the end of this journey.

We speak about pleasure and different levels of pleasure. We speak about dropping really deep into our body, living a turned-on life and enjoying Life to the fullest. We speak about orgasm as a healing modality and discovering orgasm as our birthright. It is a lot. But is it all? No, it is not.

Why are we developing our orgasm? Why are we dropping into our eroticism and orgasmicness? Why is it important? Is it only about living a happier life? This is wonderful, but, in fact, it is rather a side effect.

Speaking about sexuality and orgasm, we can focus solely on cultivation of pleasure and more pleasure and totally forget that through orgasmic expansion we are dropping deeper into ourselves. We are coming into our power. We are accessing a deeper potential of what this human experience can look like, what it actually is designed for.

At the core of liberation into orgasm is orgasm into liberation.

The tantric view of embracing Life to the fullest, of not hiding, of living totally, is not there only to give us some things to think about, ideas that are only good for the mind. The mind will never make us free. We need to go beyond it. The ultimate orgasm is when you become so big, nothing can limit you.

The ultimate orgasm is when you are expanding beyond the mind, beyond any concept, any conditioning, any trauma.

It is where there is no shame, no blame and no guilt.

You are expanding into your true Self, which has always been only whole and complete. You are having a direct realization that you have never needed anything from the outside.

The ultimate orgasm is freedom.

This is the truth of who you really are.

And yes, you can orgasm into that.

Even the smallest experiences of orgasm are the times when we are getting glimpses of who we truly are. The monkey of the mind stops jumping from thought to thought, you drop into a deep silence. You meet your Self in surrender. You become the empty silence, and you experience what it is like to be filled.

How magnificent is that. How magnificent you are. How magnificent is absolute freedom, where there are no problems to solve.

Who we think we are is limited by our conditioning.

Who we truly are is vast, eternal, timeless.

Who we truly are is one who is unborn and who alone is.

By orgasming, by cultivating orgasmicness, we are becoming more and more free. We are embodying more and more freedom. The ultimate orgasm is the orgasm into liberation where you have not just occasional glimpses of this vastness, but it becomes your reality — absolute bliss, absolute expansion becomes the background of your life.

This is the absolute orgasm. And this is absolutely possible.

Biography

Sofia Sundari is an international Tantra teacher, an author, a thought leader, founder of the Priestess School and a facilitator of courses on Tantric and Taoist sexuality.

Sofia invites her students to question beliefs that are deeply ingrained in society that block us from experiencing all of Life and being free. These are beliefs about the nature of our sexuality, emotions, relationships and Life in general.

She offers an alternative to confused mindsets and habits, and empowers people to align with their Spirit and expand into erotic freedom.

Sofia creates a space in which our darkness is no longer shameful, but where it actually nourishes our light. This is a place where spirituality and sexuality are one.

With five years in Asia studying the secrets of Tantra and Taoism and over a decade of training in various healing and spiritual modalities, Sofia has dedicated her Life to serving love.

Sofia was born and grew up in Russia. She left in 2010 when

she moved to India and Thailand. Since 2014, Sofia has been traveling the world guided by the light of her mission of activating sacred erotic temples.

For those who want to go deeper into the teachings and practices presented in this book, Sofia has created various programs: the Priestess School (an in-depth three-year course of study for women), Tantra trainings for men, women and couples as well as her online courses.

Please visit Sofia's website, www.sofiasundari.com where you can find more details about her schedule and numerous free articles and videos as well as free mini e-courses on the subject of tantric sexuality.

Liberation into Orgasm

Acknowledgements

The book wouldn't be complete without offering acknowledgements to all the beings who in a way or another contributed to the material of this book. You know who you are. Thank you for supporting me, for teaching me, for learning from me, for sharing your lives with me and for assisting me in my research. :)

I especially want to acknowledge:

Hubert who helped me open so many portals by loving me so fiercely.

Deva who was supporting me in the birthing process of this book with his shining Presence.

Life for teaching me all that I know.

Thank you for loving me. Without your love none of this would be possible.

Liberation into Orgasm

Liberation into Orgasm

28784524R00119

Made in the USA
Columbia, SC
17 October 2018